First World War
and Army of Occupation
War Diary
France, Belgium and Germany

1 DIVISION
Divisional Troops
Welsh Regiment
1/6th Battalion Pioneers
1 June 1916 - 1 April 1919

WO95/1256/3

The Naval & Military Press Ltd
www.nmarchive.com
Published in association with The National Archives

Published by

The Naval & Military Press Ltd

Unit 10 Ridgewood Industrial Park,

Uckfield, East Sussex,

TN22 5QE England

Tel: +44 (0) 1825 749494

www.naval-military-press.com

www.nmarchive.com

This diary has been reprinted in facsimile from the original. Any imperfections are inevitably reproduced and the quality may fall short of modern type and cartographic standards.

© **Crown Copyright**
Images reproduced by permission of The National Archives, London, England, 2015.

Contents

Document type	Place/Title	Date From	Date To
Heading	WO95/1256/3 6 Ba Welsh Reg Jun 16-Aug 19		
Miscellaneous	1st Division Divisional Troops 1-6th Battalion Welsh Regiment 1916 June-1919 Aug From 38 DE 1 Div		
Miscellaneous	1st Divisional Troops. Battalion Came from 3rd Infantry Brigade 15.5.16 Pioneers 1/6th Battalion Welsh Regiment June 1916		
War Diary	Maroc	01/06/1916	30/06/1916
Heading	War Diary 6th Battn. The Welsh Regiment. July 1916		
Miscellaneous	Messages And Signals.		
War Diary	Maroc	01/07/1916	02/07/1916
War Diary	Houchin	03/07/1916	31/07/1916
Heading	1st Divisional Troops 1/6th Battalion Welsh Regiment (Pioneers) August 1916		
War Diary	Baizieux	01/08/1916	14/08/1916
War Diary	Fricourt Wood	15/08/1916	19/08/1916
War Diary	Fricourt	20/08/1916	20/08/1916
War Diary	Fricourt Wood	21/08/1916	31/08/1916
Miscellaneous	A Form. Messages And Signals		
Heading	1st Divisional Pioneers 1/6th Battalion Welsh Regiment (Pioneers) September 1916		
War Diary	Fricourt Woods	01/09/1916	13/09/1916
War Diary	Bazieux	14/09/1916	18/09/1916
Miscellaneous	Fricourt Woods	19/09/1916	19/09/1916
Miscellaneous	Bazentin	20/09/1916	28/09/1916
War Diary	Fricourt Woods	29/09/1916	30/09/1916
Heading	1st Divisional Pioneers Pioneers 1/6th Battalion Welsh Regiment October 1916		
War Diary	Fricourt Wood	01/10/1916	31/10/1916
Miscellaneous		15/11/1916	15/11/1916
Miscellaneous	D.A.G. G.H.Q. 3rd Echelon	16/11/1916	16/11/1916
Heading	1st Divisional Pioneers 1/6th Battalion Welsh Regiment (Pioneers) November 1916.		
War Diary	Fricourt & Bazentin Le Petit	01/11/1916	30/11/1916
Heading	1st Divisional Pioneers 1/6th Battalion Welsh Regiment (Pioneers) December 1916.		
War Diary	Bazentin Le Petit	01/12/1916	31/12/1916
Heading	1st Division Divisional Troops 1/6th Welsh Regt, from 1st January To 31st December 1917		
War Diary	Bazentin Le-Petit Millencourt	01/01/1917	31/01/1917
War Diary	Millencourt Mericourt Sur Summe Camp 52 C Becquincourt Dompierre	00/02/1917	00/02/1917
War Diary	Dompierre Assevillers Villers Carbonnel	01/03/1917	31/03/1917
War Diary	Villers-Carbonnel Marly Camp Mericourt Sur-Somme Roisel	01/04/1917	30/04/1917
War Diary	Roisel Villers-Faucon Neuve Eglise Steen Werck	01/05/1917	31/05/1917
War Diary	Steenwerck Berthen Dickebusch Staple Dunkerque Oust-Dunkerque	01/06/1917	30/06/1917
War Diary	Oost-Dunkerque-Bains Rosendael St Pol-Sur-Mer Le Clipon Camp	01/07/1917	31/07/1917
War Diary	Le Clipon Camp	01/08/1917	31/08/1917

Miscellaneous	Le Clipon Camp Oost-Dunkerque Bains	01/09/1917	30/09/1917
War Diary	Le Clipon Camp Oost-Dunkerque Bains	01/09/1917	30/09/1917
War Diary	Oost-Dunkerque Bains Rosendael. Dambre Camp. Brielen	01/10/1917	31/10/1917
War Diary	Brielen Elverdinghe Proven.	01/11/1917	30/11/1917
War Diary	Proven Boesinghe	01/12/1917	31/12/1917
Heading	1st Division War Diaries 6th Welsh Regt. From 1st January, To 31st December 1918		
War Diary	Boesinghe	01/01/1918	31/01/1918
War Diary	Boesinghe Turco Huts	01/02/1918	28/02/1918
War Diary	Turco Huts	01/03/1918	31/03/1918
Heading	1st Divisional Pioneers 1/6th Battalion The Welsh Regiment (Pioneers) April 1918		
War Diary	Turco Huts. Bethune Beuvry Sailly Labourse.	01/04/1918	30/04/1918
War Diary	Sailly Labourse	01/05/1918	31/05/1918
War Diary	Sailly Labourse	01/06/1918	30/06/1918
War Diary	Sailly Labourse	01/07/1918	31/07/1918
War Diary	Sailly Labourse Pernes	01/08/1918	31/08/1918
War Diary	Arras area St Quentin area	01/09/1918	30/09/1918
War Diary	Berthaucourt Bohain La Valle Mulatre	01/10/1918	31/10/1918
War Diary	La Vallee Mulatre La Grand Fayt Shrs Poteries Hestrud Bossu Lez Walcourt Fraire Flavion Onhaye	01/11/1918	30/11/1918
War Diary	Mount Gauthier Haid Baillonville Tohogne Viller Ste Gertrude Vaux Chavanne Regne Bovigny SchonBerg Kronenberg Schmidtheim Munsteriefle Stotzheim Ersdorf + Altendorf	01/12/1918	31/12/1918
Heading	1919 Western Division Late 1st Division 6th Bn Welsh Regt Jan-Aug 1919		
War Diary	Ersdorf Altendorf	00/01/1919	00/01/1919
War Diary	Ersdorf Altendorf	01/02/1919	23/03/1919
War Diary	Ersdorf Altendorf	01/03/1919	23/03/1919
War Diary	Sechtem	24/03/1919	31/03/1919
War Diary	Sechtem Germany	01/04/1919	00/06/1919
War Diary	Sechtem Trippels-Dorf.	00/07/1919	00/08/1919

WO95/1256/3

6 Bn Welsh Reg

Jun 16 – Aug 19

**1ST DIVISION
DIVISIONAL TROOPS**

1-6TH BATTALION
WELCH REGIMENT
JUN — DEC 1916
—
~~Dec 1918~~

1916 JUNE — 1919 AUG

From 3 BDE 1 DIV

1st Divisional Troops.

Battalion came from 3rd Infantry Brigade 15.5.16.

PIONEERS

1/6th BATTALION WELCH REGIMENT ::: JUNE 1916.

WAR DIARY
or
INTELLIGENCE SUMMARY.

Army Form C. 2118.

1/6 Welch Reg.
Vol 12

Came from 3rd Bat.
15.5.16

P/1

9.C
29 sheets

Place	Date	Hour	Summary of Events and Information	Remarks and references to Appendices
MAROC	16/5/16		Fine day. Trench Maintenance Party worked as usual. Small party completed wire entanglements. Very little movement by our Artillery in the evening.	

Army Form C. 2118.

WAR DIARY
or
INTELLIGENCE SUMMARY.
(Erase heading not required.)

Instructions regarding War Diaries and Intelligence Summaries are contained in F. S. Regs., Part II. and the Staff Manual respectively. Title pages will be prepared in manuscript.

Place	Date	Hour	Summary of Events and Information	Remarks and references to Appendices
MAROC	2/9/16		Fine day. New defences of CALONNE consisting of Trench Maintenance Party continued work in trench. Send Ronald party for duty from Reserve Battalion.	
	3/9/16		Fine day. Continuation of work by parties. Enemy artillery & own very quiet.	

Army Form C. 2118.

WAR DIARY
or
INTELLIGENCE SUMMARY.
(Erase heading not required.)

Place	Date	Hour	Summary of Events and Information	Remarks and references to Appendices
MAROC	4/3/16		Xmas day. Continuation of work to front. Colonel Chas Beck spent Indeep Division awarded Military Cross. D.C.M. to Sgt Major Daigh and Sergt Irwin. Spent Evans slightly wounded. Our Artillery active during the day.	

Army Form C. 2118.

WAR DIARY
or
INTELLIGENCE SUMMARY.
(Erase heading not required.)

Instructions regarding War Diaries and Intelligence Summaries are contained in F. S. Regs., Part II. and the Staff Manual respectively. Title pages will be prepared in manuscript.

Place	Date	Hour	Summary of Events and Information	Remarks and references to Appendices
MAROC	5/6/16		Showery. Nothing of importance happened. Shelling on both sides very quiet.	

Army Form C. 2118.

Instructions regarding War Diaries and Intelligence Summaries are contained in F. S. Regs., Part II. and the Staff Manual respectively. Title pages will be prepared in manuscript.

WAR DIARY
or
INTELLIGENCE SUMMARY.
(Erase heading not required.)

Place	Date	Hour	Summary of Events and Information	Remarks and references to Appendices
MAROC	6/4/16		Sent S.E.R. forces from Reserve Battalion working parties carried on as usual. Enemy fired a few rounds of heavy artillery into CALONNE - also Artillery active. Wet day	

Army Form C. 2118.

WAR DIARY
or
INTELLIGENCE SUMMARY.
(Erase heading not required.)

Instructions regarding War Diaries and Intelligence Summaries are contained in F. S. Regs., Part II. and the Staff Manual respectively. Title pages will be prepared in manuscript.

Place	Date	Hour	Summary of Events and Information	Remarks and references to Appendices
MAROC	7/4/16		Small working parties out during the day doing demolition work at CALONNE. Much harrassing enemy machine gun very active throughout day. New Lewisons found front trench garrison.	

Army Form C. 2118.

WAR DIARY
or
INTELLIGENCE SUMMARY.
(Erase heading not required.)

Instructions regarding War Diaries and Intelligence Summaries are contained in F. S. Regs., Part II. and the Staff Manual respectively. Title pages will be prepared in manuscript.

Place	Date	Hour	Summary of Events and Information	Remarks and references to Appendices
MAROC	3/9/16	Atch day.	Construction of work. Enemy very quiet	

Army Form C. 2118.

WAR DIARY
or
INTELLIGENCE SUMMARY.
(Erase heading not required.)

Place	Date	Hour	Summary of Events and Information	Remarks and references to Appendices
MAROC	9/9/16		Fine day. 16 company of 12th Works (Pioneer) attached to the Unit for instruction. Spent taken over trench Battalion from Royal Engineers. Continuators of work in CALONNE and trench line. Trenches in CALONNE rather heavily shelled.	

Army Form C. 2118.

WAR DIARY
or
INTELLIGENCE SUMMARY.
(Erase heading not required.)

Instructions regarding War Diaries and Intelligence Summaries are contained in F. S. Regs., Part II. and the Staff Manual respectively. Title pages will be prepared in manuscript.

Place	Date	Hour	Summary of Events and Information	Remarks and references to Appendices
MAROC	1/4/16		Wet. Lieuts H. Morris & E.G. Morris joined and from Bureau. Continuation of work. Nothing of importance happened.	

Army Form C. 2118.

Instructions regarding War Diaries and Intelligence Summaries are contained in F.S. Regs., Part II. and the Staff Manual respectively. Title pages will be prepared in manuscript.

WAR DIARY
or
INTELLIGENCE SUMMARY.
(Erase heading not required.)

Place	Date	Hour	Summary of Events and Information	Remarks and references to Appendices
MAROC	1/8/16	Wet	Our artillery active. Continuation of work. Spent all night carrying from Reserve battalion.	

Army Form C. 2118.

WAR DIARY
or
INTELLIGENCE SUMMARY.
(Erase heading not required.)

Instructions regarding War Diaries and Intelligence Summaries are contained in F. S. Regs., Part II. and the Staff Manual respectively. Title pages will be prepared in manuscript.

Place	Date	Hour	Summary of Events and Information	Remarks and references to Appendices
MAROC	12/6/16		Wet. Construction of w.o.R. Artillery which side unpaved	

Army Form C. 2118.

WAR DIARY
or
INTELLIGENCE SUMMARY.
(Erase heading not required.)

Instructions regarding War Diaries and Intelligence
Summaries are contained in F. S. Regs., Part II.
and the Staff Manual respectively. Title pages
will be prepared in manuscript.

Place	Date	Hour	Summary of Events and Information	Remarks and references to Appendices
VROE	15/4/16		Shelled Lonsvaux front R sub to our shed from several parts of the trenches. Our French mortars and artillery reply very much CALONNE in the afternoon.	

Army Form C. 2118.

WAR DIARY
or
INTELLIGENCE SUMMARY.
(Erase heading not required.)

Instructions regarding War Diaries and Intelligence Summaries are contained in F. S. Regs., Part II. and the Staff Manual respectively. Title pages will be prepared in manuscript.

Place	Date	Hour	Summary of Events and Information	Remarks and references to Appendices
MARCQ	14/6/16		Nil. Continuation of work. Except firing thenceforward actss.	

T2134. Wt. W708—776. 500000. 4/15. Sir J. C. & S.

Army Form C. 2118.

WAR DIARY
or
INTELLIGENCE SUMMARY.
(Erase heading not required.)

Instructions regarding War Diaries and Intelligence Summaries are contained in F. S. Regs., Part II. and the Staff Manual respectively. Title pages will be prepared in manuscript.

Place	Date	Hour	Summary of Events and Information	Remarks and references to Appendices
MAROC	13/6/16		Quiet. Continuation of work. Enemy aircraft guns showed great activity against our aircraft. Stokes guns and trench mortars again busy on the line. Works were advanced one hour at dawn on 14/6/16.	

Army Form C.-2118

WAR DIARY
or
INTELLIGENCE SUMMARY
(Erase heading not required.)

Place	Date	Hour	Summary of Events and Information	Remarks and references to Appendices
MAROC	16/6/16		Cloudy day. Enemy very quiet. Continuation of work in Calonne. Nothing of importance occurred.	

Army Form C.-2118

WAR DIARY
or
INTELLIGENCE SUMMARY
(Erase heading not required.)

Instructions regarding War Diaries and Intelligence Summaries are contained in F. S. Regs., Part II. and the Staff Manual respectively. Title Pages will be prepared in manuscript.

Place	Date	Hour	Summary of Events and Information	Remarks and references to Appendices
MAROC	17/5/16		Fine day — Enemy artillery + trench mortars very active. Our working party (R.Cy.) on the left of Hyde Park was shelled, work being delayed for about an hour. Fortunately there were no casualties.	

WAR DIARY
or
INTELLIGENCE SUMMARY

Place	Date	Hour	Summary of Events and Information	Remarks and references to Appendices
MARGC	18/9/16		The Bn. headed in the Railway Cutting at 10 Am. (Chuck parade) afterwards carried on with the work in Calonne. Eight enemy aeroplanes passed going East, one was driven down by one of our 'planes. Great activity by our airmen during the evening	

Army Form C.-2118

WAR DIARY
or
INTELLIGENCE SUMMARY

(Erase heading not required.)

Instructions regarding War Diaries and Intelligence Summaries are contained in F. S. Regs., Part II. and the Staff Manual respectively. Title Pages will be prepared in manuscript.

Place	Date	Hour	Summary of Events and Information	Remarks and references to Appendices
MAROC	19/6/16		Cloudy day — A party of Officers & NCOs commenced a Revising Course at Houchin; they go down every day by motor bus returning to Maroc every evening. Working parties continued in Calonne. Very quiet day.	

Army Form C. 2118

WAR DIARY
or
INTELLIGENCE SUMMARY

(Erase heading not required.)

Instructions regarding War Diaries and Intelligence Summaries are contained in F.S. Regs, Part II. and the Staff Manual respectively. Title Pages will be prepared in manuscript.

Place	Date	Hour	Summary of Events and Information	Remarks and references to Appendices
MAROC	20/6/16		Fine day — Work continued in Calonne sector. Enemy trench mortars very active during the morning. Our Artillery very busy in the evening	

Army Form C. 2118

WAR DIARY
or
INTELLIGENCE SUMMARY
(Erase heading not required.)

Place	Date	Hour	Summary of Events and Information	Remarks and references to Appendices
MAROC	21/3/16		Fine day — Owing to motor Bus breaking down, party did not go to Noeux for instruction. Work continued in Colony. Very quiet day.	

Army Form C. 2118

WAR DIARY
or
INTELLIGENCE SUMMARY
(Erase heading not required.)

Instructions regarding War Diaries and Intelligence Summaries are contained in F. S. Regs., Part II. and the Staff Manual respectively. Title Pages will be prepared in manuscript.

Place	Date	Hour	Summary of Events and Information	Remarks and references to Appendices
	22/6/16		Fine sunny day — Work continued in Calonne. Very quiet day. German aircraft very active.	

Army Form C. 2118

WAR DIARY
or
INTELLIGENCE SUMMARY
(Erase heading not required.)

Instructions regarding War Diaries and Intelligence Summaries are contained in F. S. Regs., Part II. and the Staff Manual respectively. Title Pages will be prepared in manuscript.

Place	Date	Hour	Summary of Events and Information	Remarks and references to Appendices
	23/6/16		Heavy thunderstorm in afternoon. Work continued in Colonne. Our trench mortars very busy. Our men dug out four R.G.A. men who were buried in a house near the welling, two were alive.	

WAR DIARY
or
INTELLIGENCE SUMMARY

Army Form C. 2118

Place	Date	Hour	Summary of Events and Information	Remarks and references to Appendices
	24/3/16		Wet day. Work continued. Artillery active on both sides. Artillery trench mortars very active on both sides. Our machine guns were used nearly all day, also great activity in the air. Our Artillery bombard the German lines heavily for ½ an hour in the evening	

Army Form C. 2118

WAR DIARY
or
INTELLIGENCE SUMMARY
(Erase heading not required.)

Place	Date	Hour	Summary of Events and Information	Remarks and references to Appendices
	28/6/16		Fine day. Work continued. Another lively day; work was delayed for half an hour in the afternoon, owing to heavy German shelling in Colonne.	

WAR DIARY
or
INTELLIGENCE SUMMARY

Army Form C. 2118

Place	Date	Hour	Summary of Events and Information	Remarks and references to Appendices
MAROC	26/9/16		Wet day — "Stouchin" Officers N.C.O.s returned to duty. Fairly quiet day, but our artillery bombarded German lines in evening. A few German shells were dropped in Maroc during the night, without doing much damage.	

Army Form C. 2118

WAR DIARY
or
INTELLIGENCE SUMMARY
(Erase heading not required.)

Instructions regarding War Diaries and Intelligence Summaries are contained in F. S. Regs., Part II. and the Staff Manual respectively. Title Pages will be prepared in manuscript.

Place	Date	Hour	Summary of Events and Information	Remarks and references to Appendices
MAROC	3/6/16		Fine day — Another party of Officers & NCOs shared a course of instruction at Dieval. Quiet day but during the night we bombarded the German lines heavily for four hours. The German bombarded our lines in front of S. Maroc, heavily for 1½ hours.	

Army Form C. 2118

WAR DIARY
or
INTELLIGENCE SUMMARY
(Erase heading not required.)

Place	Date	Hour	Summary of Events and Information	Remarks and references to Appendices
MAROC	28/6/16		Wet day - 150th Continued. Very quiet day, but is bombarded the German lines for half an hour during the evening	

Army Form C. 2118

WAR DIARY
or
INTELLIGENCE SUMMARY

(Erase heading not required.)

Instructions regarding War Diaries and Intelligence Summaries are contained in F. S. Regs., Part II. and the Staff Manual respectively. Title Pages will be prepared in manuscript.

Place	Date	Hour	Summary of Events and Information	Remarks and references to Appendices
MAROC	29/8/16		Fine day — German trench mortars & artillery bombarded our lines heavily for about ten minutes at 6 o'clock P.M. MAROC was shelled a little during the night	

1875 Wt. W593/826 1,000,000 4/15 J.B.C. & A. A.D.S.S./Forms/C. 2118.

Army Form C. 2118

WAR DIARY
or
INTELLIGENCE SUMMARY
(Erase heading not required.)

Instructions regarding War Diaries and Intelligence Summaries are contained in F.S. Regs., Part II. and the Staff Manual respectively. Title Pages will be prepared in manuscript.

Place	Date	Hour	Summary of Events and Information	Remarks and references to Appendices
MAROC	30/6/16		Fine day — Our artillery shelled the enemy at intervals throughout the day. At 8-30 P.M. we shelled the Germans very heavily for about 3/4 hr. During the evening Maroc was shelled, three or 4 our billets being hit twice. Fortunately we had no casualties.	

Pioneers.
1st Div.

6th BATTN. THE WELSH REGIMENT.

J U L Y

1 9 1 6

Army Form C. 2118

MESSAGES AND SIGNALS.

No. of Message.

Prefix... Code... Words... Charge... | Office of Origin and Service Instructions... | This message is on a/c of: Service. (Signature of "Franking Officer.") | Recd. at ...... m. Date ...... From ...... By ......

TO { Adjt 1st Devons

Sender's Number | Day of Month | In reply to Number | AAA

MBM 170 2/8/16 | Kindly please War Diary for the 9 July 1916. Could you please instruct me as to the disposal of the Typescript Copy.

R.O. Bulger Capt
LIEUT. COLONEL,
COMMDG. 6TH (GLAM) BATT. THE WELCH REGT.

From ......
Place ......
Time 9.35 am

The above may be forwarded as now corrected.
Censor. Signature of Addressee or person authorised to telegraph in his name.

(Z)

10.C
32 while

6/ Welch Regt

Vol 13

continued a
for our gun
enemy very heavily

[stamp: 6th WELCH REGT]

Place | Date | Hour
MAROC | 1/7/16 |

Army Form C. 2118

1/6 Welsh Regt

Vol 13

10.C
32 while

Place	Date	Hour	Summary of Events and Information	Remarks and references to Appendices
MAROC	17/6		Fine day — Fairly quiet day. 15th continued as usual. During the night we could hear our guns a few miles away bombarding the enemy very heavily.	

Place	Date	Hour	Summary of Events and Information	Remarks and references to Appendices
MAROC	2/7/16		Fine day - Engineering course terminated. The Bn had orders to prepare to move to Hersin on the following day - 15e bombarded the German lines heavily for half an hour in the evening.	

Army Form C. 2118

WAR DIARY
or
INTELLIGENCE SUMMARY

(Erase heading not required.)

6TH BATTALION,
THE
WELSH REGIMENT.

Place	Date	Hour	Summary of Events and Information	Remarks and references to Appendices
HOUCHIN	3/7/16		Fine day — the Bn. marched from MAROC to HOUCHIN in the afternoon	

WAR DIARY
or
INTELLIGENCE SUMMARY

(Erase heading not required.)

Army Form C. 2118

Place	Date	Hour	Summary of Events and Information	Remarks and references to Appendices
HOUCHIN	4/7/16		Wet afternoon — The Bn. had a quiet day only having bathing parades their inspections etc.	

Army Form C. 2118.

WAR DIARY
or
INTELLIGENCE SUMMARY.
(Erase heading not required.)

Place	Date	Hour	Summary of Events and Information	Remarks and references to Appendices
Hovellins	5/7/16		Fine day. Battalion went for a route march in the morning	

Army Form C. 2118.

WAR DIARY
or
INTELLIGENCE SUMMARY.
(Erase heading not required.)

Place	Date	Hour	Summary of Events and Information	Remarks and references to Appendices
	6/7/16		The Bearer moved from Flesselles to Forgeville arriving at the latter place at 10 p.m. the men striking well to the accompaniment of the Regimental march Capt J.H. Gaiton & Lieut R.G.M.K. Stubbs joined the Bearer here from England. We entrained at midnight arriving at DOULLENS in the early morning	

Instructions regarding War Diaries and Intelligence Summaries are contained in F. S. Regs., Part II. and the Staff Manual respectively. Title pages will be prepared in manuscript.

Army Form C. 2118.

WAR DIARY
or
INTELLIGENCE SUMMARY.
(Erase heading not required.)

Instructions regarding War Diaries and Intelligence Summaries are contained in F. S. Regs., Part II. and the Staff Manual respectively. Title pages will be prepared in manuscript.

Place	Date	Hour	Summary of Events and Information	Remarks and references to Appendices
	7/7/16		Marched to VIGNACOURT arriving about 2 o'clock. It was a tiring march and the men enjoyed the evening rest.	

T2134. Wt. W708—776. 500000. 4/15. Sir J. C. & S.

Army Form C. 2118.

WAR DIARY
or
INTELLIGENCE SUMMARY.
(Erase heading not required.)

Instructions regarding War Diaries and Intelligence Summaries are contained in F. S. Regs., Part II. and the Staff Manual respectively. Title pages will be prepared in manuscript.

Place	Date	Hour	Summary of Events and Information	Remarks and references to Appendices
	5/1/16		At night the Battalion moved off for ST GRATIEN arriving there about 1 a.m.	

Army Form C. 2118.

WAR DIARY
or
INTELLIGENCE SUMMARY.
(Erase heading not required.)

Instructions regarding War Diaries and Intelligence Summaries are contained in F. S. Regs., Part II. and the Staff Manual respectively. Title pages will be prepared in manuscript.

Place	Date	Hour	Summary of Events and Information	Remarks and references to Appendices
	1/7/16		A quiet time and a good rest	

T2134. Wt. W708—776. 500000. 4/15. Sir J. C. & B.

Army Form C. 2118.

WAR DIARY
or
INTELLIGENCE SUMMARY.
(Erase heading not required.)

Instructions regarding War Diaries and Intelligence Summaries are contained in F. S. Regs., Part II. and the Staff Manual respectively. Title pages will be prepared in manuscript.

Place	Date	Hour	Summary of Events and Information	Remarks and references to Appendices
	19/4		There was an opportunity being competitors found	

T2134. Wt. W708-776. 500000. 4/15. Sir J. C. & S.

Army Form C. 2118.

WAR DIARY
or
INTELLIGENCE SUMMARY.
(*Erase heading not required.*)

Instructions regarding War Diaries and Intelligence Summaries are contained in F. S. Regs., Part II. and the Staff Manual respectively. Title pages will be prepared in manuscript.

Place	Date	Hour	Summary of Events and Information	Remarks and references to Appendices
	11/7/16		Another quiet day. We received four new from the line.	

Place	Date	Hour	Summary of Events and Information	Remarks and references to Appendices
	19/7/16		The Battalion received early orders to move A+B Companies proceeded by motor lorries at 7-30 am for DERNANCOURT. 150 men under Capt Sturdy proceeded in the evening as a wiring party to consolidate newly found round N.W. of CONTALMAISON. B+D Coys left ST GRATIEN at 10 am marching to BELLVUE FARM to assist in clearing the battlefield.	

WAR DIARY
or
INTELLIGENCE SUMMARY

Army Form C. 2118

Place	Date	Hour	Summary of Events and Information	Remarks and references to Appendices
	13/7/16		2 Companies proceeded to CONTALMAISON for working, remaining two Companies being engaged in road mending, mending achings the working parties experienced favourable shelling, but returned without casualties. 2 Companies A + C Companies remained at BELLVUE FARM while B + D Companies were billetted in dug-outs in O.B.I.	

Army Form C. 2118

WAR DIARY
or
INTELLIGENCE SUMMARY
(Erase heading not required.)

Place	Date	Hour	Summary of Events and Information	Remarks and references to Appendices
	13/7/16		B & D companies worked on the road and at SCOTTS REDOUBT in comparison with A & C companies continued with the work of the consolidation of the village. B & D companies suffered casualties through gas shells; three have since died.	

6th BATTALION
THE
WELSH REGIMENT.

Army Form C. 2118

WAR DIARY
or
INTELLIGENCE SUMMARY

(*Erase heading not required.*)

Place	Date	Hour	Summary of Events and Information	Remarks and references to Appendices
	15/7/16		Aerial work was very active. Was witnessed from yesterday with good results.	

WAR DIARY or INTELLIGENCE SUMMARY

Army Form C. 2118

Place	Date	Hour	Summary of Events and Information	Remarks and references to Appendices
	16/7/16		The artillery was not so much in evidence to-day. "A" Company left at night to act as a bomb carrying for the 3rd Brigade during the party, however, was held by the Divis[ion] as support. There was a very heavy scrap in front of MAMETZ WOOD. "B" & "D" Companies sent out all night and captured BLACKWATCH ALLEY. They were heavily shelled going through CONTALMAISON but fortunately there were no casualties.	

WAR DIARY
or
INTELLIGENCE SUMMARY
(Erase heading not required.)

Army Form C. 2118

Instructions regarding War Diaries and Intelligence Summaries are contained in F. S. Regs., Part II. and the Staff Manual respectively. Title Pages will be prepared in manuscript.

Place	Date	Hour	Summary of Events and Information	Remarks and references to Appendices
	17/7/16		Our guns were very busy this evening. A & B Companies repaired the road beyond CONTALMAISON while C & D Companies worked in front of the trenches N.E. of CONTALMAISON.	

Place	Date	Hour	Summary of Events and Information	Remarks and references to Appendices
	18/7/16		C & D companies carried on the same as yesterday, while B & D companies continued the wiring of the front line. They were heavily shelled N of CONTALMAISON. Capt J.R. Donaldson-reed, attached to the Battalion	

WAR DIARY
or
INTELLIGENCE SUMMARY
(Erase heading not required.)

Army Form C. 2118

Instructions regarding War Diaries and Intelligence Summaries are contained in F. S. Regs., Part II. and the Staff Manual respectively. Title Pages will be prepared in manuscript.

Place	Date	Hour	Summary of Events and Information	Remarks and references to Appendices
	19/7/16		Headquarters & C & C Companies moved to ALBERT. The four companies left at 6 p.m. to make a new front line trench between POIZIER and BAZENTIN-LE-PETIT wood. The move was successfully carried out. The 2nd and 3rd Brigades supplied the burying parties. 6 Companies found badly in returning through CONTALMAISON. One shell killing 8 men and wounding 7.	

6th BATTALION,
THE
WELSH REGIMENT.

Place	Date	Hour	Summary of Events and Information	Remarks and references to Appendices
	30/7/16		The Battalion tonight proceeded to dig a 2½ ft trench between GLOSTER TRENCH & MUNSTER TRENCH. Orders made for the purpose of serving those who were to make the attack on POZIER. The work was carried out satisfactorily in spite of the fact that we were in close proximity to the enemy. Our losses were only 4 wounded casualties.	

WAR DIARY or INTELLIGENCE SUMMARY

Army Form C. 2118

Place	Date	Hour	Summary of Events and Information	Remarks and references to Appendices
	21/7/16		We continued work on the newly made trench started by the LOYAL NORTH LANCS. The enemy shelled CONTALMAISON road very heavily. 2 Lieut S. D. Edwards was wounded in the head through shrapnel. There were also 4 other non-com casualties.	

WAR DIARY or INTELLIGENCE SUMMARY

Army Form C. 2118

Place	Date	Hour	Summary of Events and Information	Remarks and references to Appendices
	22/7/16		Tonight there is an attack on the SWITCH LINE. 3 Companies we attached to the 2nd Brigade and one to the 1st Brigade. Our part was to follow up the advance and dig communication trenches between JONES TRENCH & the SWITCH LINE. However, as the attack was unsuccessful there was very little consolidation to be done. Capt Crosby was wounded while waiting in the trench for the work to be done. 2/Lieut Evans attached to the 14th GLOSTERS reconnoitred WELSH ALLEY right up to within 20 yards from where the German front trench branched off. He then formed a barricade to prevent any surprise sortie of the enemy down this trench. 2/Lieut Baden Jones did meritorious work among the enemy wounded.	

6th BATTALION, THE WELSH REGIMENT

WAR DIARY
or
INTELLIGENCE SUMMARY

Army Form C. 2118

Place	Date	Hour	Summary of Events and Information	Remarks and references to Appendices
	23/7/16		The day was one of rest for R.E. Companies. It was noticed that many of the civilian population of ALBERT were beginning to return. B & D Companies continued work up at SHELTER WOOD	

WAR DIARY
or
INTELLIGENCE SUMMARY

Place	Date	Hour	Summary of Events and Information	Remarks and references to Appendices
	24/2/16		A + C companies moved from ALBERT to the Old British reserve line, while D Company took up trenches with HQ at ALBERT. B Coy went into trenches at SHELTER WOOD. The C.O. went into Hospital with trench fever and Capt. & Adjutant took over the command of the Battalion	

WAR DIARY
or
INTELLIGENCE SUMMARY

(Erase heading not required.)

Army Form C. 2118

Place	Date	Hour	Summary of Events and Information	Remarks and references to Appendices
	25/1/16		B Company continued trench digging. 6 Company made a big effort to carry on to a 3ft 6in french trench but were hindered considerably by the enemy's fire	

WAR DIARY
or
INTELLIGENCE SUMMARY

Army Form C. 2118

Place	Date	Hour	Summary of Events and Information	Remarks and references to Appendices
	26/7/16		The Battalion goes out to rest. Company after assembling at ALBERT for an hour to BAIZIEUX received orders to proceed that night to CONTAINMAISON to make another attempt to make a communication trench but again the work was made impossible by the enemy capturing the French but again the work was made impossible through the very heavy shelling by the enemy. The Battalion less this Company marched to BAIZIEUX (WOOD) a distance of some 10 Kilometres from ALBERT.	

Place	Date	Hour	Summary of Events and Information	Remarks and references to Appendices
	27/7/16		Company joined the Battalion at BAIZIEUX and the Battalion on reaching their Billets were granted 48 hours well deserved rest.	

Army Form C. 2118

WAR DIARY
or
INTELLIGENCE SUMMARY
(Erase heading not required.)

Instructions regarding War Diaries and Intelligence Summaries are contained in F. S. Regs., Part II. and the Staff Manual respectively. Title Pages will be prepared in manuscript.

Place	Date	Hour	Summary of Events and Information	Remarks and references to Appendices
	28/7/16		The men have settled down and appear to appreciate the rest.	

6th BATTALION,
THE
WELSH REGT

WAR DIARY
or
INTELLIGENCE SUMMARY

Army Form C. 2118

Place	Date	Hour	Summary of Events and Information	Remarks and references to Appendices
	29/7/16		In reality is all has carried by digging C.T.s & bombing posts at the end of then 48 hours rest and physical drill, bomb practice, and instruction in field defences.	

Date	Hour	Summary of Events and Information	Remarks and references to Appendices
30/7/16		The Battalion carried out the same programme as yesterday. In the afternoon an invitation was received from 10th Brigade for the officers and men to attend the Brigade sports.	

Place	Date	Hour	Summary of Events and Information	Remarks and references to Appendices
	31/7/16		The weather is still gloriously fine. Physical drill, Company drill, etc, occupied the morning. In the afternoon there was a General inspection by Major General Strickland, G.O.C. 1st Division of the new draft of R.W.F's & 37 March.	

1st Divisional Troops

1/6th BATTALION

WELCH REGIMENT (Pioneers)

AUGUST 1916

Army Form C. 2118

WAR DIARY
or
INTELLIGENCE SUMMARY
(Erase heading not required.)

1/4 Welsh Regt
Vol 14

11.C
33 sheets

Place	Date	Hour	Summary of Events and Information	Remarks and references to Appendices
BAIZIEUX	1/8/16		The hot & bracing continental weather which is truly ideal and the wounded receive the magnificence of their summer glow, made a glorious resting place. We were rocked to sleep by a trio of dim airmen who were speedily driven off by our own vigilant men. Sgt Robinson was admitted to Hospital this day. The Companies were taken on arriving and divisional training of sand marching.	

6th BATTALION
THE
WELSH REGIMENT
No............
Date............

WAR DIARY
or
INTELLIGENCE SUMMARY

Army Form C. 2118

8th BATTALION,
THE
WELSH REGIMENT

Place	Date	Hour	Summary of Events and Information	Remarks and references to Appendices
BAIZIEUX	25/6		Today the Battalion & the 1st Divl. Engineers were inspected at HENENCOURT WOOD on their return from BAIZIEUX by Lieut Gen. Sir H.P. Pulteney K.C.B. D.S.O. the 3rd Corps Commander who welcomed us in to his corps as a known Battalion & in the course of a felicitous speech which had the ring of genuine sincerity paid our units a high tribute such arduous and difficult tasks in the work of consolidation had been accomplished by both Divisions standing around Ovillers-Mouquet subsequently the Battalion under the command of Capt. F.H.S. Winton gave an admirable march past, the General again beaming much pleasure. Today 2/Lieuts Brown & Barker Jones left us for the R.F.C. The Battalion lose two good officers.	

WAR DIARY
or
INTELLIGENCE SUMMARY

Army Form C. 2118

6th BATTALION
THE WELSH REGIMENT.

Place	Date	Hour	Summary of Events and Information	Remarks and references to Appendices
BRIZIEUX	3/8/16		The morning was occupied, some Platoons in drill, having the musketry ms of trenches. Havig 2 officers & men from each Company, representing a Platoon, a Company left for a spot near HENENCOURT, to practise with Battalions of the 3rd Brigade the wearing & giving of signals to aeroplanes in an advance, by means of red rockets. The demonstration was very successful. Some rumours made another appearance today, to announce that the Division was going to India. The men were mainly find the fellow who replied with nothing to do in "INDIA".	

WAR DIARY
or
INTELLIGENCE SUMMARY

Army Form C. 2118

Place	Date	Hour	Summary of Events and Information	Remarks and references to Appendices
BAIZIEUX	4/9/16		The morning was spent in drill & running and in the afternoon, the Division held a very successful horse show at HENENCOURT. We won a third in the relay race	

8th BATTALION
THE
WELSH REGIMENT.

Place	Date	Hour	Summary of Events and Information	Remarks and references to Appendices
BAIZIEUX	5-8-16		We held battalion sports in the aerodrome field. The function was very enjoyable. Brig. Gen. Pears attended. The weather was again magnificent and during the afternoon there was some spirited events. Pride of place in the programme was taken in the competition for the best squad of men. The event hanging much interest. The first was awarded by Capt. Gwilym to the Lewis Gunners in the horse race, HUSSAR ridden by Sgnd. Ed. L. Owens the transport officer was the winner. In the evening we carried "H" She 34th Div. supply at the Boxing competition. Sanger'd "H" She 34th Div. supply between Pte Tommy Phillips, our young Welsh champion, forced Sgt Robinson of the Camerons to give up in the seventh round, whilst Pte Austin Sidon scored hundreds over their men.	

WAR DIARY
or
INTELLIGENCE SUMMARY

Army Form C. 2118

Place	Date	Hour	Summary of Events and Information	Remarks and references to Appendices
BAIZIEUX	6/8/16		Parties from A & B Companies left for ALBERT to dig deep dugouts. It appeared that since we left that place had been very heavily shelled. The day being Sunday, the rest of the Battalion attended Divine Service. There is a continuation of magnificent weather and the rear is being hugely enjoyed. 2nd Lieut Cowley received his temporary captaincy this date.	

Army Form C. 2118

WAR DIARY
or
INTELLIGENCE SUMMARY

(Erase heading not required.)

Instructions regarding War Diaries and Intelligence Summaries are contained in F. S. Regs., Part II. and the Staff Manual respectively. Title Pages will be prepared in manuscript.

Place	Date	Hour	Summary of Events and Information	Remarks and references to Appendices
BAIZIEUX	7.9.16		Royal went in again. More Bosche here for ALBERT today, but A & D Coys made capital targets with dug outs. B Coy left for HENENCOURT on road when going for R. Coy refreshing the Battalion were inspected by the C.R.E. in transport field. Rumours we shall be fighting about the air. The latest — We are to Police Paris. This evening the acting C.O. received his Majority.	

WAR DIARY
or
INTELLIGENCE SUMMARY

Army Form C. 2118

Place	Date	Hour	Summary of Events and Information	Remarks and references to Appendices
BAIZIEUX	1.8.16		One big day out almost confined to ALBERT. C Coy. parked on the road toward HENENCOURT. B Coy had the day for baths. The M.O. announced to us that the limits for name and its mood had reached S.J.Q.	

6th BATTALION
THE WELSH REGIMENT.

WAR DIARY
or
INTELLIGENCE SUMMARY

Army Form C. 2118

Place	Date	Hour	Summary of Events and Information	Remarks and references to Appendices
BAIZIEUX	9-8-16		Good work resumed at ALBERT. R.E. Officers approved plans with the road work at HENENCOURT which is being carried on by B & C Coys. Capt Dodsworth admitted to Hospital Thursday.	

8th BATTALION,
THE
WELSH REGIMENT

WAR DIARY
or
INTELLIGENCE SUMMARY

(Erase heading not required.)

Army Form C. 2118

Place	Date	Hour	Summary of Events and Information	Remarks and references to Appendices
BAZIEUX	16th		Rain for the first time since we entered the trenches. B & C Coys obtained road work at HENENCOURT, A & B Coys fell out went into ALBERT. Notification of recommendation for tests for hawks Roberts Rowlen for RFC received.	

6th BATTALION,
THE WELSH REGT

WAR DIARY
or
INTELLIGENCE SUMMARY

(Erase heading not required.)

Army Form C. 2118

Place	Date	Hour	Summary of Events and Information	Remarks and references to Appendices
BAIZIEUX	11-8-16		The arrangements made at ALBERT by A & Q. bays are admirable. No complaints have been received. Training & road work continued at HENENCOURT by B & C Coys. Lieut. Roberts left for Flying Corps & has accepted as a pilot & should Roberts as an observer, the latter returned to the unit for a fortnight.	

WAR DIARY
or
INTELLIGENCE SUMMARY

(Erase heading not required.)

Army Form C. 2118

Place	Date	Hour	Summary of Events and Information	Remarks and references to Appendices
BAIZIEUX	19/6/16		Notification received that the rest period draws to a close in a couple of days. Everyone has benefited by the stay. With the exception of drills & runs in the morning the time was given to rest.	

Army Form C. 2118

WAR DIARY
or
INTELLIGENCE SUMMARY

(Erase heading not required.)

Place	Date	Hour	Summary of Events and Information	Remarks and references to Appendices
BAIZIEUX	19/6/16		The C.O. Lt.Col C.A.S.Gunston D.S.O. will resume command this Sunday after his absence in hospital. Divine Service were held. Orders received to move.	

WAR DIARY or INTELLIGENCE SUMMARY

Army Form C. 2118

6th BATTALION, THE WELSH REGIMENT.

Place	Date	Hour	Summary of Events and Information	Remarks and references to Appendices
BAIZIEUX	14/8/16		Rained heavily in morning during B & C Coys route march left for BECOURT WOOD, in the outskirts of ALBERT. The marching was heavy, but the men stuck it well. The dinner is certainly a great help. We bivouacked in the open but fortunately the rain kept off during the night, and we are deuced well. "I have a Great companying and an altruistic officer in the morning." Johnen like a lotta kandots, slug a nice cold bath, he did wash, mannages two sticky clothes.	

WAR DIARY
or
INTELLIGENCE SUMMARY

Army Form C. 2118

Place	Date	Hour	Summary of Events and Information	Remarks and references to Appendices
FRICOURT WOOD	15/8/16		The Batt: less the C.M. Stores & transport which remained at BECOURT WOOD, & D Coy which remained for road work at ALBERT, left FRICOURT WOOD at 10.30 a.m. for bivouacs in FRICOURT WOOD, relieving the North Staffs. The interior of the wood came in for intermittent shelling, there had come survived the man. Similar observation seems to have a number of accurate but in several men were observed there to remain all night having enough to show we would imagine, and still ~~the~~ giving information. Coy very badly informed. Bodies, number high as C Coy were moving up very indifferently to enforce. Coy very indifferently very loose men there on the ridge of the subject showing through through two megaphones a few other emergency thro' mens a court. C Coy was attached to the by Brigade to B Coy & D Coy to the 2nd R.Sc.F. Coys left at 7.30 to dig a new forward trench, facing MARTINPUICH. It was a bright moonlight night. The Black Watch accompanied Clery. The right position for C Coy was to the enemy & there to enplane machine guns. The Blackwatch were very able to get out as Company. The enemy observed the right position & kept men being fire where they fix heavy to the approaches. Despite this seven to the Coy	

WAR DIARY
or
INTELLIGENCE SUMMARY

(Erase heading not required.)

Army Form C. 2118

Place	Date	Hour	Summary of Events and Information	Remarks and references to Appendices
B			wounded to aid on the left position. Worked on the right had to be abandoned. We suffered 15 killed & 3 wounded, one of the latter being Sergt. T.B. Jones, who being our with the Battalion. B Coy was engaged in marking a "enemy's" redoubt off WATERTRENCH in HIGH WOOD facing the left of MARTIN PUICH. This Company also came under heavy fire but accomplished its task. The man who killed one wounded - Sergt J. Evans was also found and whilst attending to the wounded man, the Coy. Sustained loss a splendid officer. This is the second occasion in which Sergt Evans who as an Engineer surveyor was approvably adapted to the work has been put out of action. A Coy and good work in digging a communication trench behind B Coy. They returned without any casualties. The evening is making a stubborn defence	

WAR DIARY
or
INTELLIGENCE SUMMARY

(Erase heading not required.)

Army Form C. 2118

Place	Date	Hour	Summary of Events and Information	Remarks and references to Appendices
FRICOURT WOOD	16/8/16		Our men are in good spirits despite a fairly severe shelling time. Boy tp + two mining Lieutenants held returns it day to improve communication trench & by to deepen the shallow trench behind the front line in the position of the ground right. The "OP" or "Dug-Out" reporting that Boches with unreliable fuzes + "dummies" attacks are being exploded into a mishap in which our few wounded generally ran from our lines to fill their billets + getting creaphoric sounds to mean an attack. In the interim another liaison with officials line and raises its for watches or man more quickly back to supports. Repetitions of these "stunts" keep the time for the proper attack. The commun while a moveing and shotings. The Companies returned without any casualties with the exception of one slightly wounded man in C Coy	

WAR DIARY
or
INTELLIGENCE SUMMARY

(Erase heading not required.)

Army Form C. 2118

Place	Date	Hour	Summary of Events and Information	Remarks and references to Appendices
FRICOURT WOOD	17/5/16		Our Artillery which has been very busy with bursts of bombardments gave a warm about this morning. Boches returned same in the neighbourhood of FRICOURT WOOD and one man seen to be seriously wounded and brought down in the neighbourhood of Co.H.Q. MAISON. 2nd Lt M.H. Pym took up duties of Bomb Officer to 3rd Brigade Mushrooming. No night the Cont. abattis continued to continual work. C Coy clearing fair & opening communication trench in same position. 13 Coy and further admirable work under the direction of Capt. Hull on the Redoubt. The Coys returned without any casualties.	

WAR DIARY
or
INTELLIGENCE SUMMARY

Army Form C. 2118

Place	Date	Hour	Summary of Events and Information	Remarks and references to Appendices
FRICOURT WOOD	16/8/16		The Division is having a very hard time. The Boche is making a determined effort to seize the Wood. His artillery seems to be as strong as our artillery. His communication between his front line & his guns is complete. His return strength of own artillery must however be in/to nil to Co. The 2nd Brigade to secure all its objectives taking however but the 1st Brigade is being badly knocked about and no fresh North of the MinDmpe. C Coy is attacked. Communicades C Coy is unable to entrench its road if Consolidation two wiring. A & B Coy proceed as a covering party to dig a communication trench which has appeared trenched HIGHWOOD)	

WAR DIARY
or
INTELLIGENCE SUMMARY

Army Form C. 2118

Place	Date	Hour	Summary of Events and Information	Remarks and references to Appendices
FRICOURT WOOD	19/8/16		Ordered at 3.30am by Capt Cowley, O.C. B. Coy to take two Company Sufford H.Q. Instructions named to gain information thereto. M/g the Windmill. The hard dead. Work could not with loss of men killed & wounded. A + B Coy went heavily shelled during the evening which carried out with bayonet assist. There were 5 crumps wounded amongst these. No other are nothing behind HIGHWOOD. The officer of men is obtained 3my & met further good progress communication trenches behind captured trench at HIGHWOOD. 2nd/Lt. Coy. Lost Lieut Buckfield who received a slight wound above the stomach. In event of it was that he was taken for a spy + anyone who knows this officer + his dress of ingenious schemes for aging the enemy of the situation. He was escorted by a retinue of Officers to his Battn H.Q. at FRICOURT WOOD where 'hyph' was placed on the subject. It is not intended to publish the movements of the para 2/Lieut H.H. Buckfield.	

6th BATTALION,
THE
WELSH REGIMENT.

WAR DIARY
or
INTELLIGENCE SUMMARY

(Erase heading not required.)

Army Form C. 2118

Place	Date	Hour	Summary of Events and Information	Remarks and references to Appendices
FRICOURT	30/1/16		The 1st Brigade to which 6 Coy had been attached took over Sunday. C Coy left duty in the morning to go where sub. Coy knew of under heavy shelling but happily no casualties. The Coy was very pleased to retire from trenches at H.G.S Hoay. This morning A & C Coys were augmented by detail thrown by the Adjutant for further digging of communication trench. The enemy shelled us heavily at the shelter. We are otherwise having Rifles etc. but other than [illegible] of action yesterday few losses.	

6th BATTALION
THE
WELSH REGIMENT.

WAR DIARY
or
INTELLIGENCE SUMMARY

Army Form C. 2118

Place	Date	Hour	Summary of Events and Information	Remarks and references to Appendices
FRICOURT WOOD	21/8/16		FRICOURT WOOD visited this morning with entrenching accoutrements from Minor Girmi Road, by a large party of men armed with entrenching tools from Minor Girmi Cay in the line this evening that Companys having been moved forward to a strong point on the left of HIGHWOOD. The Enemy guns are percistently shelling this good wood who dire this afternoon otherwise proceeded. Capt. Edwards admitted to Hospital this day.	

Army Form C. 2118

WAR DIARY
or
INTELLIGENCE SUMMARY

(Erase heading not required.)

Place	Date	Hour	Summary of Events and Information	Remarks and references to Appendices
FRICOURT WOOD	22/8/16		Further unusual activity over FRICOURT WOOD this day. ALBERT a calling B Coy who are left to continue road to Fricourt Wood being today for distribution among the troops. Such a proceed at an important point this morning and showing it units previous at an important point this morning and showing a draft of 36 joined the Batn this evening. B Coy proceeded to covering C Coy's work in the strong front. Guard of honor sharing the situation of ruined S.O.S. Own Batt is in excellent spirits. Today we received a notice that their officers gave an admirable production of a light age turning gun in use CO's with has been received in the city of Arras. No recently all are to prepare as will those finding little find time in who tried to make up a Battalion we are marching Friday	

Army Form C. 2118

WAR DIARY
or
INTELLIGENCE SUMMARY
(Erase heading not required.)

Instructions regarding War Diaries and Intelligence Summaries are contained in F. S. Regs., Part II. and the Staff Manual respectively. Title Pages will be prepared in manuscript.

Place	Date	Hour	Summary of Events and Information	Remarks and references to Appendices
FRICOURT WOOD	23/8/16		An unfortunate happening that marred the continued good progress of work occurred last night. Guides of "D" coy got lost with the result that the position could not be found, & the party returned without having done any work. Early this morning A & b coy left to repair roads on the route leading from the cutting at CONTAL MAISON to MAMETZ. There was some capital work was done. "A" coy returned early. "B" coy returned in the latter part of the afternoon in which the new draft received its baptism admirably. A party from "A" & "D" coy left this evening to make a new trench in the Wood of HIGHWOOD. They did some capital work despite the fact that they were subjected to very heavy shelling. "A" coy lost two Officers wounded. — 2nd Lt R. Brown & 2nd Lt I.W. Jacob. 2 ORs killed & 7 ORs wounded. "D" coy lost 2 ORs wounded.	

Army Form C. 2118

WAR DIARY
or
INTELLIGENCE SUMMARY
(Erase heading not required.)

Place	Date	Hour	Summary of Events and Information	Remarks and references to Appendices
FRICOURT WOOD	2/9 3/9/16		The "Division" is "holding". The weather is bad. 2nd Lieut Pte Routley took a party from "C" coy early this morning for work in conjunction with the Engineers, on the making of a light railway on a track leading from the road which is in front of BAZENTIN LE GRAND, to the front line. The rest of this company proceeded with road work on the CONTALMAISON - MAMETZ route, behind the support trenches. Much artillery strength is being exhibited by the enemy, who is throwing his best into this all important part of the line.	

Army Form C. 2118

WAR DIARY
or
INTELLIGENCE SUMMARY
(Erase heading not required.)

Instructions regarding War Diaries and Intelligence Summaries are contained in F.S. Regs., Part II. and the Staff Manual respectively. Title Pages will be prepared in manuscript.

Place	Date	Hour	Summary of Events and Information	Remarks and references to Appendices
BECOURT WOOD	25/8/16		D'Coy with details last night & early this morning made further good progress with the new trench, and during this work took two prisoners. Casualties Two Other Ranks killed and four wounded. "C" Coy proceeded early to-day to continue the making of the CONTALMAISON–MAMETZ road. Good progress made. There was considerable aerial activity on both sides, & the enemy exhibited good shooting in adjacent dteries. A message was distributed from the Commander in Chief congratulating the Division on its work. It is having a difficult time to during this period the enemy is making his premier effort. The Battn. heard with satisfaction that the Medical Officer (Capt. W.A. Sneath) had received the Military Cross. None is unanimous tribute to its merit, and an associated eulogy that the decoration which has been for too long delayed, is a deserved reward for meritorious service in the field.	

Army Form C. 2118

WAR DIARY
or
INTELLIGENCE SUMMARY
(Erase heading not required.)

Instructions regarding War Diaries and Intelligence Summaries are contained in F. S. Regs., Part II. and the Staff Manual respectively. Title Pages will be prepared in manuscript.

Place	Date	Hour	Summary of Events and Information	Remarks and references to Appendices
FRICOURT WOOD	24/9/16		"B" Coy returned this morning with good report of continuous work done on Dam'd position. "C" Coy left early with two parties, one under Smith the Routley for continuation of work on light railway, and another under Spalding & M. Morgan for work on CONTALMAISON - MAMETZ road. Nothing of note this date. "D" Coy at night, deepened 150 yards of trench West of new trench, off CLARKS trench	

1875 Wt. W593/826 1,000,000 4/15 J.B.C. & A. A.D.S.S./Forms/C. 2118.

WAR DIARY
or
INTELLIGENCE SUMMARY

(Erase heading not required.)

Army Form C. 2118

Place	Date	Hour	Summary of Events and Information	Remarks and references to Appendices
FRICOURT WOOD	9/8/16		Capt. T.C. Irwin & Capt. T.C. Wills returned from hospital today. "C" Coy installed many huts of CONTALMAISON - MAMETZ road. "A" Coy took over "D" Coys work at night.	

WAR DIARY
or
INTELLIGENCE SUMMARY

Army Form C. 2118

Place	Date	Hour	Summary of Events and Information	Remarks and references to Appendices
FRICOURT WOOD	8/9/16		"A" Coy returned early morning with good report of their progress. "B" Coy took over "C" Coys road work. The batln Coomfrang went out to make dugouts in the support trenches right of HIGH WOOD. "A" Coy with half of "C" Coy & details proceeded to dig an advanced support trench about ten yards behind the front line on the fringe of HIGH WOOD. Good work carried out, but the enemy spotted the party & were subjected to heavy fire.	

WAR DIARY
or
INTELLIGENCE SUMMARY

(Erase heading not required.)

Army Form C. 2118

Place	Date	Hour	Summary of Events and Information	Remarks and references to Appendices
FRICOURT WOOD	29/9/16		"A" Coy continued this dugouts. The weather is very bad, but it has not deterred the spirits of the men. News that Romania is "joining up" is heartening. "D" Coy left to improve ELGIN AVENUE Trench, right of HIGH WOOD. In coming away Sgt Myrddin Jones, a brother of Sgt J.B. Jones who was promoted recently, was caught & struck by a bit of shrapnel, and died instantly. His death takes away another soldier from the original number of a member of a family that has seen much service in the Unit, the father being a Colour Sergt when the Unit was the 3rd V.B. Volunteers.	

6th BATTALION,
THE
WELSH REGIMENT.

WAR DIARY
or
INTELLIGENCE SUMMARY

Army Form C. 2118

(Erase heading not required.)

Instructions regarding War Diaries and Intelligence Summaries are contained in F. S. Regs., Part II. and the Staff Manual respectively. Title Pages will be prepared in manuscript.

Place	Date	Hour	Summary of Events and Information	Remarks and references to Appendices
FRICOURT WOOD	30/9/16		Capt. J. L. Bradby, Capt. F. L. Mills, & their 2/Lt D. R. Thomas reconnoitred ground around HIGH WOOD in case of developments. "D" Coy resumed road work & "C" Coy made progress in dugouts. 2nd Lieut. P. G. Routley took a party of "A" Coy at night to connect a forward trench at HIGH WOOD. The weather has been very bad the last few days, but the Division is maintaining as somewhat spirit under trying conditions. The trenches are leg deep in many parts in water and the roads are in a quagmire state.	

1875 Wt. W593/826 1,000,000 4/15 J.B.C. & A. A.D.S.S./Forms/C. 2118.

WAR DIARY
or
INTELLIGENCE SUMMARY
(Erase heading not required.)

Army Form C. 2118

Place	Date	Hour	Summary of Events and Information	Remarks and references to Appendices
FRICOURT WOOD	31/4/16		A return of Donohue, 31/4/16 in advance today, our visit area FRICOURT. The Battalion has been up for 7 days, and reviewing the work it took have been fulfilled with results that are satisfactory, showing a further demonstration of the general adaptability of the men to manifold work of a varied character. They have exhibited tenacious traits under, I on many occasions, trying circumstances, but have well maintained a reputation decidedly gained in a period in France & Belgium, that now makes 22 months.	

9TH BATTALION
THE WELSH REGT

9TH BN (GLAM) BATT: THE WELSH REGT

"A" Form.
MESSAGES AND SIGNALS.

Army Form C.2121 (in pads of 100).

TO: Adro Div.

Sender's Number: AM 97 438
Day of Month: 2-9-16

AAA

for Seventh month please War Diary of August 1916

Lieut. Colonel
Comdg 6th (Glam Batt. Welsh Regt.)

1st Divisional Pioneers

1/6th BATTALION WELCH REGIMENT (PIONEERS)

SEPTEMBER 1916.

WAR DIARY or INTELLIGENCE SUMMARY

Army Form C. 2118

6th Welsh Regt.

Vol 15

Place	Date	Hour	Summary of Events and Information	Remarks and references to Appendices
FRICOURT WOODS	1916 Sept. 1st		6th Battalion The Welsh Regiment. The advent of the autumn. What will it bring? There appears to be considerable tension in the East. Here the Huns' artillery strength is still still, but as we are in the all important sector, and the "Land of the Push", we cannot form a criterion. To the normal observer though, it is obvious that in the air we hold a complete mastery. The countryside is dotted with guns, but, above all and everything, the spirit of all ranks is magnificent, and remains, below anything, the one great key to open wide the gate of victory. To-day, "A" Coy. proceeded to improve the road leading from HIGH ALLEY to THISTLE ALLEY; "B" Coy. from MACMAHON BRIDGE; and "D" Coy. on the dug-outs, in front of WINDMILL; and "C" Coy., in platoon shifts, on new dug-outs in ELGIN AVENUE and THISTLE AVENUE. In the afternoon, the enemy replied sharply to our guns, and put much shrapnel on and h.e. on incoming troops. "A" Coy. lost five o.r. killed, and ten wounded. "C" Coy. last shift came in for heavy fire also, on taking up positions, and work was delayed in THISTLE AVENUE. Both parties from this Coy. completed the tasks	

L. Abraham
72.C
Bombers

Place	Date	Hour	Summary of Events and Information	Remarks and references to Appendices
FRICOURT WOODS (continued)	Sept 1st (continued)		sometime after midnight, but was troubled by enemy gas shells, and on leaving through the valley, was caught in a barrage. The Huns exhibited a wily tactic in bombarding with unknown gas shells, and following quickly with h.e.; an evident intention to stampede troops and make them take off their helmets. Our men behaved very commendably; but one o.r. had to be left at a dressing station. The march fell the effects in a minor way.	

WAR DIARY
or
INTELLIGENCE SUMMARY

(Erase heading not required.)

Army Form C. 2118

Place	Date	Hour	Summary of Events and Information	Remarks and references to Appendices
FRICOURT WOODS	Sept 2nd		"D" Coy continued work on dug outs, and "A" Coy and "C" detachment on roads. The rest of "B" Coy at ALBERT resumed their road work. It was an uneventful day, a peace before a storm.	

Army Form C. 2118

WAR DIARY or INTELLIGENCE SUMMARY

Place	Date	Hour	Summary of Events and Information	Remarks and references to Appendices
FRICOURT WOODS	Sept 3rd		Today the 1st Brigade grouped made a big assault on HIGH WOOD. Big preparations were made. Two gun caps were allotted positions in readiness to dig fire saps to the captured German line. The parties being unfortunates. In cover 300 "zero" splendidly included, a variety of shell, trench mortars, liquid fire, and machine guns, made lighter, an intense bombardment. The brigade, with the Camerons and Black Watch in front, supported by the Gloucesters and Welch, dashed over in a fog of smoke, caused by the mammoth fire, the blowing up of three mines, and the liquid fire. It was a terrible exhibition of modern warfare in all its heinous intensity, demoralising to anything mortal, and enough to cow the spirits of the bravest. But the repetition of close assaults on the same narrow area has prepared the Huns, who replied with all the strength of his guns, and brought up supports from natural above, and redoubts. They kept their positions. Captain L.C. FRISBY with 12 men, proceeded from the front line to Sap C to commence work as soon as the infantry has	

Place	Date	Hour	Summary of Events and Information	Remarks and references to Appendices
FRICOURT WOODS (continued)	Sept 3rd (continued)		had been blown. He behaved with characteristic gallantry, spurring his men on to big efforts. Repeated attempts were made by the enemy to drive him out to his left party in the bomb fights, remaining at his post with a heroic stoicism. He was able to carry out his objective & the threatened rush to his own safety, which he completely disregarded. One bullet pierced through his helmet, another through his coat, but he was able to get back with nothing more than a slight concussion in the head. The remainder of the party performed good and splendid work in clearing and deepening the much shelled HIGH ALLEY, THISTLE ALLEY, FRASER TRENCH, and BLACK WATCH TRENCH. One party also carried 50 live bombs to the Gordons and the Camerons. The rest of the battalion marched afterwards in squads, and continued work on the dugouts in front of the WINDMILL. We were again a lucky battalion in our losses of casualties, which were two O.R. killed and 11 wounded, which took Hills two wounded.	

Army Form C. 2118

WAR DIARY
or
INTELLIGENCE SUMMARY
(Erase heading not required.)

Place	Date	Hour	Summary of Events and Information	Remarks and references to Appendices
FRICOURT WOODS (continued)	Sept. 4th		To-day, "B" Coy. carried on the work, with "B" Coy. left. "C" clearing falls in HIGH ALLEY, ELGIN AVENUE, and BLACKWATCH TRENCH, whilst "D" Coy. made excellent progress on the dug-outs. At ALBERT, much good work was resumed, together with the loading and unloading of material. The Battalion is continued good resumé, now experiencing a hard time, which it bore with a magnificent spirit. The Bn. Wr. to-day received the following congratulatory order :— "The Divisional Commander wishes to express to you his admiration of the conduct of the Brigade yesterday. The fact that they did not retain the position they had captured, which was very heavily counter-attacked, does not in the least detract from the great gallantry with which they assaulted. Please convey his remarks to all troops concerned." The Brigadier message was as follows :— "The Brigadier desires to express his thanks to all ranks for their part in the preparations and fighting of yesterday. In spite of having no rest for three weeks, and being under severe bombardment most of the time, the	

WAR DIARY
or
INTELLIGENCE SUMMARY

Place	Date	Hour	Summary of Events and Information	Remarks and references to Appendices
FRICOURT WOODS (continued)	Sept 4th (continued)		spirit of the officers and men was excellent, and deserved better luck than I had into the enemy's lines. The Brigadier very much regrets the heavy casualties incurred, but feels certain that those losses will be avenged in the next battle with the same spirit that has always predominated in this brigade, and calls for the praise from the Divisional Commander: " he an enthusiastic attendance to our Commanding Officer, the Brigadier states: - " The enclosed order includes your battalion, which has always done good work for us, and helped us in every way. I hear that the party under Capt. Frosby, in Sap C, were simply splendid, specially Frosby himself. Please convey to him and his party our admiration of their conduct. (sd) A.W. Peddie." Lieut. F.J. Hinton, the bulk of the second in command, was admitted to hospital today.	

Army Form C. 2118

WAR DIARY or INTELLIGENCE SUMMARY

Place	Date	Hour	Summary of Events and Information	Remarks and references to Appendices
FRICOURT WOODS (continues)	Sept. 5th		"A" Coy and "B" Coy. worked on roads from FLAT IRON COPSE to THISTLE ALLEY, and "D" Coy on the roads. "C" Coy cleaned huts in ELGIN AVENUE. Three men were sent to ALBERT, the rest of "B" Coy completed 80 yards of road, and 80 yards of Sunken road. 7/Lt-C. Rowley received a slight shell wound in the head whilst working on the roads with his L.M.G. team. The men are all working very hard.	

6th BATTALION THE WELSH REGIMENT

WAR DIARY
or
INTELLIGENCE SUMMARY

Army Form C. 2118

Place	Date	Hour	Summary of Events and Information	Remarks and references to Appendices
FRICOURT WOOD I (continued)	Sept 6th		The Coys. continued road work, and "A" Coy in clearing falls in HIGH ALLEY. Food was received at ALBERT. It was an uneventful day. The enemy continues his consistent shelling, but there was much aerial work on our side.	

Place	Date	Hour	Summary of Events and Information	Remarks and references to Appendices
PRICOURT WOODS (continued)	Sept 9th		The Battalion continues a very hard task. In every branch of the service, a unity of big effort is being exhibited. Today "A" Coy works on tunnel S3d 9.6.6 to S3d 2.0.6., deepening to an average depth of 8 ft 6 ins. "B" Coy continued work on dug outs; "C" Coy made good progress on new trench S.W. of HIGH WOOD. The Battalion shows a fine determined spirit under heavy fire, which is continuous during their operations. Casualties, one O.R. killed and one wounded.	

WAR DIARY
or
INTELLIGENCE SUMMARY

Army Form C. 2118

Place	Date	Hour	Summary of Events and Information	Remarks and references to Appendices
FRICOURT WOODS (continued)	Sept 8th		"A" and "D" Coy continued the consolidation — "A" Coy on trench from S3d 9.5½ to S4c 1½, and D Coy on trench from S3d 6 9 to within FIFE ALLEY. A draft of 80 arrived this date. Casualties 6 men, pte O.R. Cosnales — 2nd Lieut- O.K. Thomas admitted to hospital.	

Army Form C. 2118

WAR DIARY
or
INTELLIGENCE SUMMARY
(Erase heading not required.)

Place	Date	Hour	Summary of Events and Information	Remarks and references to Appendices
FRICOURT WOODS (continued)	Sept 9th		Today, the 3rd Brigade made a heavy assault on HIGH WOOD. "B" Coy, under Captain C. J. Carley, went up to the work of consolidation. Again, there was a heavy bombardment, intensified in the five minutes prior to Zero, with heavy mortars, the blowing up of mines, Lewis fire, and a rapid concentration of machine gun fire. The Munsters, 2nd Welsh, and S.W. Borderers set off with a big cheer, but despite the dynamic effort, the attack failed for reasons irrelevant in this diary. None shewed more coronation in valour than the conspicuous gallantry of Lt. Col. Palmer, Commanding Officer of the Munsters who, despite his advanced years — he was in his fifties — led his men to the lives of seven Germans with bayonet and revolver, and stuck to his captured line, though wounded in the groin, until it was necessary to take up position in the original line so as to safeguard the	

1875 Wt. W593/826 1,000,000 4/15 J.B.C. & A. A.D.S.S./Forms/C. 2118.

WAR DIARY
or
INTELLIGENCE SUMMARY

Army Form C. 2118

Place	Date	Hour	Summary of Events and Information	Remarks and references to Appendices
FRICOURT WOOD (contd)	Sept 9th (contd)		Flanks. The 2nd Welch performed heroic work in standing to their original piece of trench. "E" Coy made good work in clearing galls in HIGH ALLEY and ELGIN AVENUE, and in carrying up bombs for Cornwallis. We are one Lewis (O.R.) and five O.R. wounded. Arrival of two guns today.	

Place	Date	Hour	Summary of Events and Information	Remarks and references to Appendices
FRICOURT WOODS (continued)	Sept 10th		The Battn, augmented by a part of D Coy, "C Coy", and "A Coy", left three styles in the making of an assembly trench. — BEDFORD ST., ON HIGH ALLEY. He works was carried out with violent success, despite of times of heavy fire. "D" Coy continued work on a new trench to be used behind BEDFORD ST, as an assembly point. At ALBERT, "B" Coy made further excellent work on the roads.	

Army Form C. 2118

WAR DIARY
or
INTELLIGENCE SUMMARY
(Erase heading not required.)

Instructions regarding War Diaries and Intelligence Summaries are contained in F. S. Regs., Part II. and the Staff Manual respectively. Title Pages will be prepared in manuscript.

Place	Date	Hour	Summary of Events and Information	Remarks and references to Appendices
FRICOURT WOOD (continued)	Sept 11th		The Corps warned further good work in the trenches near our starting point, that 6 (rather later) was cleared in HIGH ALLEY and ELGIN AVENUE, which were opened (simply for the tenure). No bivouac was affecting a relief in good order; and, apparently, without executing any suspicion. There was a big influx of troops for a further big rally.	

Place	Date	Hour	Summary of Events and Information	Remarks and references to Appendices
FRICOURT WOOD	Sept 12th		Bonfanus started work on making roads up to BAZENTIN LE GRAND. At night, Lt-Quarter-Master Brown joined the Battalion from England. No Lieutenant had, for some considerable time, occupied the position of adjutant, of the lines line, with Lieut. Bastin as his assistant.	

WAR DIARY
or
INTELLIGENCE SUMMARY

Army Form C. 2118

Place	Date	Hour	Summary of Events and Information	Remarks and references to Appendices
FRICOURT WOODS (continue)	Sept 13th		Trench work continued, and preparation made for a move to BAZIEUX. It was a quiet day. 16 men being particularly Lieupd, 2nd Lieut Nicholl left to assume temporary duties of Adjt of Bois Bomb School.	

Army Form C. 2118

WAR DIARY
or
INTELLIGENCE SUMMARY
(Erase heading not required.)

6th BATTALION,
THE
WELSH REGIMENT.

Place	Date	Hour	Summary of Events and Information	Remarks and references to Appendices
BAZIEUX	Sept. 14th		The Battalion, which is now very strong, moved off for BAZIEUX. The road discipline was good, and only a couple of men fell out en route. The Unit was in Coln. reserve. Major Hinton arranged excellent billets in the village. We occupied late tonight. The weather was of the best additional kind. Lt. (Temp Capt.) Richards, & Lt. Napier, Rankin, and Harrison joined the Battalion from England.	

WAR DIARY
or
INTELLIGENCE SUMMARY

Army Form C. 2118

Place	Date	Hour	Summary of Events and Information	Remarks and references to Appendices
BAZIEUX	Sep. 15th		The day was taken for rest, cleaning, and General cleaning up.	

Army Form C. 2118

WAR DIARY
or
INTELLIGENCE SUMMARY
(Erase heading not required.)

Instructions regarding War Diaries and Intelligence Summaries are contained in F.S. Regs., Part II. and the Staff Manual respectively. Title Pages will be prepared in manuscript.

6th BATTALION,
THE
WELSH REGT.

Place	Date	Hour	Summary of Events and Information	Remarks and references to Appendices
Sgy BAZIEUX	Sept. 16th		Today the Commanding Officer gave a Lecture (and demonstration) before Officers, NCO's, & regimental instructors in drill, being the course of his lectures, he voiced a keenness over the to-work that has been performed in the line, adding that the Unit has earned a very high name. The Officers XI beat the representatives of the men at cricket. This was also some enjoyable inter Coman's Rugby and Association football.	

1875 Wt. W593/826 1,000,000 4/15 J.B.C. & A. A.D.S.S./Forms/C. 2118.

WAR DIARY
or
INTELLIGENCE SUMMARY

Army Form C. 2118

Place	Date	Hour	Summary of Events and Information	Remarks and references to Appendices
BAZIEUX	Sept. 17th		A course of training was started, opening with drill, and interspersed with wiring classes, and demonstrations in the making out of winches.	
			Lieut Norman left to join the Batt. [initials]	

Place	Date	Hour	Summary of Events and Information	Remarks and references to Appendices
BAZIEUX	Sept. 18th		News received that we are required in the Line again. There was some splendid news of further advances, which came on as a panacea for the bad news. Heavy rain set in today.	

Army Form C. 2118

WAR DIARY
or
INTELLIGENCE SUMMARY
(Erase heading not required.)

Place	Date	Hour	Summary of Events and Information	Remarks and references to Appendices
FRICOURT WOODS	Sept 19th		Another wet day, but never cleared off. When the Battalion commenced its move, the extent of the "grate mob", which has been made in very large numbers, was apparent. On our arrival at FRICOURT SPURS billets left vacant on account of evacuation from enemy barrages and gun posts, were now crowded with bivouacs & lean-to shelter. Looked out the same billets, even among billets stated to be Jones River. With an uncommon occurrence this & indeed, the huts lovely was to own handiwork, and invariably leaves a copious litter to remove its activities in some like the area	[Stamp: 6th BATTALION THE WELSH REGIMENT]

WAR DIARY or INTELLIGENCE SUMMARY

Army Form C. 2118

Place	Date	Hour	Summary of Events and Information	Remarks and references to Appendices
BAZENTIN	Sept 20th		The Battalion, less Q.M. Stores and "C" Coy., under L.M. Lawrence and Smithers left and took up billets in the trenches ON HIGH ALLEY and ELGIN AVENUE. Lieuts Akenhead, Taylor, and H. Morris, were loaned to the Grenade Supply Co. By the side of H.Q. Dug-out, being temporary dormant, were the much spoken of "tanks". They surrounding country, at night, and from an eminence, looked like a representation of some "lights of London" environs, transport, men in bivouacs, appears to take up every inch of ground. Reports in advance, and behind the walls of HIGH WOOD artillery had made them new positions, and were on hand – the just bound to come in to conquered territory – became part of this conglomeration, seemingly so chaotic, yet so orderly. Of the British machine that in such scything its path through the enemy's defences, Khead of HIGH WOOD with a performing whatever to the "sausage one" that	

WAR DIARY or INTELLIGENCE SUMMARY

Army Form C. 2118

Place	Date	Hour	Summary of Events and Information	Remarks and references to Appendices
BAZENTIN (contd.)	Sept 20th (contd.)		had a narrow shave, New Zealanders wandered about making and taking their food in the open with their songfroid - in characteristic of, which might be contrasted in her analysis of the Bulletin O[?] all a magnificent spectacle, and the pity is that strategy, in such an unparalleled line, has to give way to limited objectives. And now our cons down to the past [?] on our right:- "A", "B", and "D" Coys, resting, and commenced a winding communication trench from the much vaunted SWITCH LINE to STARFISH REDOUBT from which some Hanover Tanks [?] helped knew are might. Relieved by some Hanover Tanks. Tactful however the men (A) born to m. the new task, carried on in every part; the men (A) born to slanted depth. The initial difficulty in such works,	

Place	Date	Hour	Summary of Events and Information	Remarks and references to Appendices
BAZENTIN (continued)	Sept 20th (continued)		so cooling the greatest — the placing out of the men. 2nd Lieuts well Visits (in Leadership), that the journey was made, 2 words released with 2nd. Matheson casualties one O.R. being wounded, 2nd. Browne also receiving a slight wound. He was able to remain at duty.	

WAR DIARY or INTELLIGENCE SUMMARY

Army Form C. 2118

Place	Date	Hour	Summary of Events and Information	Remarks and references to Appendices
BAZENTIN	Sept 21st		Today, the Battalion was augmented by 'C' Coy from FRICOURT. Also the previous day this was following the full truth. Speed ordered of transport, which was landscapped on. He arrived and sited the noble transport has fallen, and in parts of the route leading to BAZENTIN LE GRAND, this was very dangerous. The enemy, who kept the Camp under continual observation from his Sausage Sables throughout the day, as usual "his attempts no where were carried his expenditure". Two lorries the Bn. proceeds to continue the work on the Communication trench, & two lorries were came under heavy fire. The men at dawn is carried work on setting to the trench, & before the completion of the task, a loss average of 5/1 yards buried width 3/1 width has been reached. Unfortunately, no suffered in casualties, five o.r. killed, and during the day, 10, the appreciable number was received by the 19 o.r. wounded. Among the dead, 2/O, near the No 5 Branch, at the corner of BAZENTIN 2/Lt Rawlinson died from a shell, 2/Lt Herbert Morris. There was no more Injuries than in the Battalion. The news cast quite a gloom.	

WAR DIARY or INTELLIGENCE SUMMARY

Army Form C. 2118

Place	Date	Hour	Summary of Events and Information	Remarks and references to Appendices
BAZENTIN	Sept 22nd		There was a return to beautiful autumnal weather, which counteracts helped the work of consolidation. Again the enemy kept up a heavy shelling and concealed artillery on main approaches. At night the Bn. left 6. dig an advance trench from DROP ALLEY. An/on fire short-was made on the top front, a length of 300 yards was reached; on the side front, 500 yards; and a flanks of 300 yards. 12am worked the ventilated trogan, and all down to an average of 3ft. 9in. and a width of 3ft. Ind: Blee haviz, Lt. Harrow was wounded in the arms by shrapnel. He was laid hold, for it was of his second night. 2Lt. Eglit. O.R. was wounded	

Army Form C. 2118

WAR DIARY
or
INTELLIGENCE SUMMARY
(Erase heading not required.)

Instructions regarding War Diaries and Intelligence Summaries are contained in F.S. Regs., Part II. and the Staff Manual respectively. Title Pages will be prepared in manuscript.

Place	Date	Hour	Summary of Events and Information	Remarks and references to Appendices
BAZENTIN	Sep. 23rd		This evening, "A" & "B" Coys. carried the finishing touches to the communication trench, and "C" & "D" Coys. to the completion of the advanced trench, which was now being taken over by the 3rd Bde. The Battalion again did praiseworthy work. There O.R. were killed, and six wounded. The stamina, determination, and excellence of spirit exhibited by the men in tasks performed under circumstances that are trying and difficult, are worthy of the highest commendation. Every effort is being made to carry out orders.	

1875 Wt. W593/826 1,000,000 4/15 J.B.C. & A. A.D.S.S./Forms/C. 2118.

Army Form C. 2118

WAR DIARY
or
INTELLIGENCE SUMMARY
(Erase heading not required.)

Place	Date	Hour	Summary of Events and Information	Remarks and references to Appendices
BAZENTIN	Sept 24th		"A" Coy pushed the advance trench this night, and "B" Coy made an excellent finish to the communication trench — CORK ALLEY. "A" & "D" Coys made an excellent mule track leading from CORK ALLEY to HIGH WOOD. The battn is having a hard time, but there is with the slightest sign of any weakness in ranks. Two O.R. wounded.	

WAR DIARY
or
INTELLIGENCE SUMMARY

Army Form C. 2118

Place	Date	Hour	Summary of Events and Information	Remarks and references to Appendices
MAZENTIN	Sept 25th		Work was resumed on making trenches and dug outs. It was an exceedingly fine day. There was heavy gunfire to our right, to our shelling continued to hold up a defence, but they were seen that he was holding. We left right our wounded this date.	

Army Form C. 2118

WAR DIARY or INTELLIGENCE SUMMARY

(Erase heading not required.)

Place	Date	Hour	Summary of Events and Information	Remarks and references to Appendices
BAZENTIN	Sept 26th		During the night the Battalion proceeded to DROP ALLEY to dig another forward trench, but it was found from the position that had been taken from the map, that to attempt it, on the ground from the position about 300 yards of the Hun lines, and, the would be making an effort which we cannot undertake, would be many between ourselves and the tanks. As I was the enemy, to its certainly very alarming. Left to tell the story. As I was the enemy, it is certainly very nerving, to another attack which we are being made a here at all hours, but-up a heavy barrage, and all attempts at work are frustrated. Although the work has successfully attempted much. This order was hardly a little too difficult. Those O.R. were killed & two wounded.	

WAR DIARY or INTELLIGENCE SUMMARY

Army Form C. 2118

Place	Date	Hour	Summary of Events and Information	Remarks and references to Appendices
BAZENTIN	Sept 27th		The Division, having made another successful local attack and gained a 600 yd [?] length of the enemy's line, quickly made a communication trench to the captured trench. Brigade reconnoitring ability was shown by Capt. T.C. Walker, with 7 head hidges, but whom had [?] in the previous raid, shown further determination. Then special aptitude for this branch of the work. The leadership of Capt. Frobes was also warmly [?], & he had now brought in 1 [?] without a single casualty. It was a splendid piece of work.	

Army Form C. 2118

WAR DIARY
or
INTELLIGENCE SUMMARY
(Erase heading not required.)

Instructions regarding War Diaries and Intelligence Summaries are contained in F. S. Regs., Part II. and the Staff Manual respectively. Title Pages will be prepared in manuscript.

Place	Date	Hour	Summary of Events and Information	Remarks and references to Appendices
BAZENTIN	Sept 25th		Tothan, the Bn., the Division having been relieved, moved back to FRICOURT, being for the time attached to the 47th Division. An uneventful day. Speculation was rife as to the future movements of the Division. It has certainly played its part on the Somme.	

Army Form C. 2118

WAR DIARY
or
INTELLIGENCE SUMMARY

(Erase heading not required.)

Instructions regarding War Diaries and Intelligence Summaries are contained in F. S. Regs., Part II. and the Staff Manual respectively. Title Pages will be prepared in manuscript.

Place	Date	Hour	Summary of Events and Information	Remarks and references to Appendices
FRICOURT WOODS	Sept. 2nd		Parties from each coy did road work from BAZENTIN coming to THISTLE AVENUE. Nothing of note to record.	

1875 Wt. W 593/826 1,000,000 4/15 J.B.C. & A. A.D.S.S./Forms/C. 2118.

Place	Date	Hour	Summary of Events and Information	Remarks and references to Appendices
FRICOURT WOODS	Sep 30th		Work was resumed on the roads, and during the day, news was received that the Division was being withdrawn, however, in a metaphorical sense, and, unluckily, with the end of the month synchronises with the close of the work on the Somme. It has been a historical period, and without trying very to hyperbole or unnecessary eulogy, it can be recorded with a certitude of truth that a fine accomplishment of a varied character, wrought with cheer daring but dogged obstinate spirited determination, has been achieved, and further lustre added to the already fair name of the little band of territorials from the haunts & hamlets of Southern & Western Wales.	

A.F.Stammell Capt
ADJT O.C. 9 Service Batt: THE WELCH REGT

1st Divisional Pioneers

PIONEERS

1/6th BATTALION WELCH REGIMENT :: OCTOBER 1916.

Army Form C. 2118.

1/6 Welsh Regt

WAR DIARY
or
INTELLIGENCE SUMMARY.
(Erase heading not required.)

1/6th Welch Regt. (T.F.)

Instructions regarding War Diaries and Intelligence Summaries are contained in F. S. Regs., Part II. and the Staff Manual respectively. Title pages will be prepared in manuscript.

Place	Date	Hour	Summary of Events and Information	Remarks and references to Appendices
FRICOURT WOOD	1.10.16 to 31.10.16		The Division was out at rest at ABBEVILLE during the month. The Battⁿ remained behind & was employed on the roads in the neighbourhood of BAZENTIN LE PETIT. The condition of the roads was extremely bad owing to the incessant rain, and only a few of the main roads are now passable. The Battⁿ started making a new camp, just in front of Fricourt Wood, but have been handicapped owing to difficulty in obtaining material. No ever sufficient AMIENS HUTS have been obtained to house half the Battⁿ, the remaining half of the Battⁿ still occupy their old bivouacs in FRICOURT WOOD. For the purpose of work the Battⁿ were attached to the C.R.E. of the 49th Division and on their relief by the 9th Division they came under the C.R.E. of that Division & finally under the supervision of the C.R.E. of the 50th Division. No event of importance occurred during the month, the work being of a similar nature throughout & consisting of repairing the damage caused to the roads by heavy vehicles, & putting down fresh metalling. A number of Officers & men have been sent to the Divisional Bomb School, to undergo a 10 days' course in Bombing. The Lewis Gun Section have been increased to 100 strong, & the new men have undergone a thorough training at the hands of the Lewis Gun Officer. The Section is now composed of 8 guns. Leave reopened during the month, on a very limited scale.	

CRE
1st Div.

The attention of the 1/6th Welsh ought to be drawn to F.S. Regs Pt II Sect. 140, which lays down how War Diaries should be kept & their purpose. The attached is not considered to conform, & is returned for the very earliest re-submission. Probably one page of A.F.C. 2118 would be sufficient, if the matter were condensed & suitably expressed.

H. Burrows. Bt Lt Col.
a/DAA & QMG 1st Div.

13.11.16.

6th Welsh
Forwarded
14/11/16

To OC 1st Division CRE.
Complied with & returned

15/11/16.

A.A.G.
G.H.Q. 3rd Echelon.

Forwarded with reference to my No. 6134. of 13"/16

H. Munro.
Bt. Lt. Col.
for Maj. Genl. Ch. 1st D

16.11.16

1st Divisional Pioneers

1/6th BATTALION WELCH REGIMENT (PIONEERS)

NOVEMBER 1916.

WAR DIARY
or
INTELLIGENCE SUMMARY
(Erase heading not required.)

Army Form C. 2118
1/6th Bn. The Welsh Regt.
Vol 17

14.C.
1 sheet

Place	Date	Hour	Summary of Events and Information	Remarks and references to Appendices
FRICOURT	1/30 Nov 1916		The Company entrained from GOOF ALLEY on the route around BAZENTIN	
BAZENTIN LE PETIT			up till the 17th. The Bn. also had rails on the 16th-17th running from PETIT BAZENTIN to BAZENTIN – LE – PETIT from Rd 3/Br Bn. 19th Bn. Coy moved into OVERLAND ROUTE on the 19th & commenced with no 1 OVERLAND ROUTE.	
			On the 19th Lord Bury, Major in command, allotted with no FRICOURT to BAZENTIN – LE PETIT. B Coy continued at FRICOURT. 3 Companies worked on OVERLAND ROUTE & continued to work till the 24th on ROUTE 9 continued to work from the 14th till 16th – 21st Cov Bn's worked with A Coy on the 18th on OVERLAND RY & from the 22nd 6 Coys Coy and the 21st to No HANGER ALLEY A Coy is band to come from lift work on HANGER ALLEY and A Coy commenced on N. 4. 3rd & No 4 OVERLAND on FISH LANE as A 2a at a round. This is said to run along a blue village pump to JUNCTION & FACTORY CORNER. C Coy LESBŒUFS Aby & continued work & OVERLAND ROUTE & continued work on ROUTE ALLEY & commenced work on & and Co. to return work in FISHLANE Blvd. Mid C Coy the move back to FRICOURT	

R. H. Owen
ADJT 6TH (GLAM) BATT THE WELSH REGT.
CAPTAIN

1st Divisional Pioneers

1/6th BATTALION WELCH REGIMENT (PIONEERS)

DECEMBER 1916.

WAR DIARY or INTELLIGENCE SUMMARY

Army Form C. 2118

1/5 Welsh Regt

15C.
1 sheet

Place	Date	Hour	Summary of Events and Information	Remarks and references to Appendices
BAZENTIN LE PETIT	1916 Dec 1/31st		The Battalion continued work on FACTORY CORNER, PIONEER ALLEY etc. Work was greatly delayed owing to the unfavorable weather conditions. On Christmas night the Battalion had a dinner which went off very well. On the 27th three Warrant Officers arrived from the Same Unit to relieve three of our warrant officers. One of the two Sergeant Majors had a bad shoot stay and he being there was newly wounded on the 30th. On two occasions the Battn Sergts held a dinner "smoker" to which the officers of the Battalion were invited. There was a great success. On the 31st the Division was relieved in the line by the 50th Division.	

R.C. Bodger Captain
6th BATTN. THE WELSH REGT.

1st/k Division

Divisional Troops

1/6th/11 Welch Regt.

From 1st January To 31st December 1917

WAR DIARY or INTELLIGENCE SUMMARY

16th Bn. The Welsh Regt. (G.F.) Vol 19

16 C 2 sheets

Place	Date	Hour	Summary of Events and Information	Remarks and references to Appendices
BAZENTIN LE PETIT — MILLENCOURT	1/1/17 to 31/1/17		The Battalion continued work in the trenches in the neighbourhood of BAZENTIN-LE-PETIT. 3 Coys. working on the roads & rack (?) boardway in excavation, undergoing a weeks training in Camp. On the 2nd Jany R.S.M. Jones J. & C.S.M. Wickham & Bate, & 2nd Lt Sergt L.S.M. Young, left for England, their places being taken by warrant officers who arrived from England at the end of December 1916. On the 9th Jany Lt. Col. Somers + on the 22nd Jany R.Q.M.S. Taylor, left for England. 2nd Lt. G.L. Buckland joined the Battalion as candidates for Commissions. The Commanding Officer, Lt Col. C.O. Bell D.S.O. went on leave on the 16th Jany & 2nd Lt. G.L. Buckland joined the Battalion the same day. The Battalion was considerably augmented by reinforcements, a draft of 102 arriving on the 10th, & the total reinforcements received during the month amounting to 162. The Battalion vacated the trenches at the end of the month & was concentrated at FRICOURT (when last records kept ended by us), being there joined by the 16th A.& B. Corps, returning to it by & on the 30th they relay, relay work, took over from Details from BAZENTIN moved to MILLENCOURT the remainder of the Battalion remaining at BAZENTIN. The 21st Brigade were together here on and	

WAR DIARY
or
INTELLIGENCE SUMMARY.

Army Form C. 2118.

Place	Date	Hour	Summary of Events and Information	Remarks and references to Appendices
(continued)				
BAZENTIN LE PETIT	11/1/17 to 31/1/17		work at BAZENTIN on the 25th & our men leaving two companies joined the remainder of the Battalion at MIRAUMONT on the 26th.	
MIRAUMONT				R.G.R. Ebergen Capt & adjt 6/Rifle Welsh Regt Commdg 6th R/Rifle Welsh Regt

WAR DIARY or INTELLIGENCE SUMMARY

Army Form C. 2118

1/6th Bn Welsh Regt (T.F.)

Vol 20

Place	Date	Hour	Summary of Events and Information	Remarks and references to Appendices
MILLENCOURT MERICOURT sur SOMME CAMP 52a BECQUINCOURT DOMPIERRE	1917		The Battn moved on the 3rd from MILLENCOURT to MERICOURT SUR SOMME into a camp recently taken over from the French & on the 5th moved on a little further to Camp 52a situated at R8c. This camp was vacated on the 7th when the Battn proceeded to the neighbourhood of DOMPIERRE & commenced work on Trench Maintenance etc. Men were retained in dugouts at BECQUINCOURT. On the 11th two moved to dugouts in a Trench at DOMPIERRE. The Battn worked on MARTINIQUE, GUADELOUPE, REUNION AVENUES and TOULON'S ALLEY. Up to about the 16th when a Rain Frost prevailed, the trenches were in excellent condition though the hard state of the ground made new advance. After the thaw which was accompanied by rain the state of the trenches was very bad and it required the greatest efforts on the part of the Battn by draining, clearing water and etc. to make them at all passable. The erection of a camouflage screen along the ASSEVILLERS - FLAUCOURT Road was commenced & trench board stands were laid. 8,10 Elephant shelters were erected at DOMPIERRE for Bn requirements. Major W.S. Brown returned from Hospital on the 9th. Lt Col 6.O.S. Evelton D.S.O. returned from leave on the 9th. Captain R.G Lindsay Macmajor M.C. proceeded on leave on the 21st. The M.O Capt S.A Smith M.C.(RAMC) who had been with the Battn since June 1915 was transferred to the Regular RAMC & joined the No.1 Bus Ambulance on the 19th his place being taken by Capt. D.S. Cooper (RAMC)	J.D. 17.C. 1 sheet [Stamp: 6th BATTALION, THE WELSH REGIMENT] 4/2/17 A.E. Curtis Lieut

WAR DIARY
or
INTELLIGENCE SUMMARY
(Erase heading not required.)

Army Form C. 2118

6th BATTALION,
THE
WELSH REGIMENT

6 Welch
13/1

No 21

Place	Date	Hour	Summary of Events and Information	Remarks and references to Appendices
DOMPIERRE ASSEVILLERS to VILLERS-CARBONNEL	1/3/17 to 31/3/17		The Battalion continued Trench Maintenance work, erection of camouflages screening etc until the 17th inst. The extensive enemy retirement which took place about this time rendered our Trench Maintenance work unnecessary. On the 19th the Batt. commenced the work of repairing roads & removing obstructions from the roads on LINE across of the SOMME. The Germans on their retreat had felled trees across the road & increased the difficulties of this by using time bombs, trenches had been dug across the roads, that were exploded so as to form craters & cross roads & other places in order that our guns should be thought up as quickly as possibly it was essential that the roads should be made passable to heavy traffic at the earliest possible moment. The Batt. responded splendidly to the call & though the work was at a considerable distance from our Billets & involved a fatiguing march, progress was made with such speed as to earn the warm approbation of the Army Commander & others. Lieut W.J. Browne was admitted to hospital & was on the 2nd sent to England. On the 6th being struck off the strength on this latter date. Capt. E.T. Michell rejoined the battn from the 1st Brit Bomb School on the 1st. The Adjt. Capt. R.C. Lindsay–Bradyer M.C. returned from leave on the 8th. On the 15th inst. the Bombing officer Lieut E.C. Carlton LAS. (D.S.O.) left the Batt. to take temporary command of the 8th Royal Berks Regt. Major L.C. Grosby M.C. taking over command of this Battn. On the 20th of Bn moved to dug-outs south of the ASSEVILLERS & on the 22nd again moved to a dug-out lately vacated by the Germans under the main AMIENS ROAD about 500 yards to the East of VILLERS CARBONNEL. On the 27th it again moved about 500 yards further East along the main road into shelters erected by the Battn at about M.29.D.6.5	

L.C. Crosby Major
LIEUT COLONEL,
COMMDG 6TH (GLAM) B THE WELSH REGT

Army Form C. 2118.

WAR DIARY
or
INTELLIGENCE SUMMARY.
(Erase heading not required.)

1/6 Welsh Regt
Vol 22
19.C
Sheet

Place	Date	Hour	Summary of Events and Information	Remarks and references to Appendices
VILLERS-CARBONNEL to MARLY CAMP MERICOURT SUR-SOMME ROISEL	1/11/17 to 30/11/17		The Battalion continued work on Road maintainance in the neighbourhood of VILLERS CARBONNEL, BELLOY & ASSEVILLERS. Work was hindered by heavy falls of snow. 2nd Lt. J.W. Davis joined the Batt. on 2/11/17. "A" & "B" Coys left VILLERS CARBONNEL on the 6th & proceeded to MARS Camp, on the CHUIGNOLLES-BRAY-SUR-SOMME road, for a period of rest & training, the other two companies continuing work on roads until the 10th when they joined the remainder of the Batt. at MARLY Camp. Major A.L. Bowen left this Batt. to join the 36th Division on the 10th. On the 13th an inspection of the Battalion was held by Major General R.G. Strickland C.B. C.M.G. D.S.O. commanding 1st Division. The Battalion left MARLY Camp on the 17th & proceeded to Camp No 5 MERICOURT SUR SOMME. Here training was continued including practice in "the normal formation for the attack" etc. Various inter. Company football matches were held & the Battalion also played matches with teams representing other Units who were stationed in the same district. Great interest was aroused by a Rugby match between teams representing this Battn. & the 8th Royal Berks (now commanded by Lt Col Baskerton D.S.O) but the result was an easy win for us by 38 points to 3 points. 2nd Lt G. Webb rejoined this Batt. on the 22nd & 2nd Lt H.B. Evans on the 25th inst. On the 26th the Battn. took part in manoeuvres with the 2nd Brigade near PROYART, the Batt. acting as a defending party against an attack carried out by 2nd Brigade. On the 30th the Battn. proceeded to ROISEL for work on railway.	

L.C. Irsby
Comm'dg 6th (GLAM) Bn : THE WELSH REGT

WAR DIARY
or
INTELLIGENCE SUMMARY.
(Erase heading not required.)

20 C.
2 sheets

Place	Date	Hour	Summary of Events and Information
ROISEL	1/5/17		The Battalion commenced work near ROISEL on the 1st May, with the Sounder Coy Troops & under the supervision of the 62nd Division, & were employed on Railway work, repairing damaged
VILLERS-FAUCON			track & preparing new track ready for the laying of rails. Much progress was made & the
NEUVE EGLISE	3/5/17		track rapidly advanced, so that it became necessary for the Battn to move to VILLERS FAUCON in order to be nearer the site of work & this was done on the 7th inst. Major Bowen A.L. on
STEENWERCK			leaving the Battn 10/4/17 presented a Silver Cup for Inter-Company Competition & arrangements were being made to hold Battn sports at which this Cup would have been awarded to the Coy attaining highest aggregate points, when orders were received for the Battn to move at short notice by train & these arrangements fell through. On the 14th inst the Battn left VILLERS FAUCON & marched to LA CHAPELETTE, via PERONNE. The Battn entrained at LA CHAPELETTE & proceeded to BAILLEUL, the scene of some of its former labours detraining there on the 15th inst & afterwards bivouacing about 2 kilometres south of NEUVE EGLISE. The Battn was then attached to the 2nd Anzac Corps for work, and was split up into numerous parties & worked on Light Railway construction, Road maintenance, Water supply & points, Gun emplacements, level crossings etc. On the 29th inst the Battn moved to a camp about 2 kilometres north of STEENWERCK

WAR DIARY
or
INTELLIGENCE SUMMARY.

Army Form C. 2118.

continuing that the work under the 2nd Anzac Corps.

News was received during the month that the Commanding Officer Major S.C. Grisby (M.C.) had been appointed acting Lieut Col as from 30th March 1917, that Capt T.R. Dowdeswell had been appointed acting Major as from the 25th April 1917. On the 21st inst a letter was received through the 1st Division from General Sir H.S. Rawlinson, Bart, KCB, KCVO, Commanding Fourth Army, expressing his appreciation of the work done by the 1st Division whilst in the Fourth Army, & his regret that on joining the XIV Corps, the 1st Division would no longer be under his command.

The following officers were mentioned in Sir Douglas Haig's dispatches during this month :- Lt Col S as Bazleton (DSO) Lt Col L.C. Grisby (M.C.) Capt R.C. Lindsay - Mahison (M.C.) Capt E.F. Cowley, Lt E.D. Cleaver Q.O.M.S. 2/S/Bennadick

J.R. Oundenell
LIEUT. COLONEL,
COMMDG 6TH (GLAM) BR. :: THE WELSH REGT.

WAR DIARY or INTELLIGENCE SUMMARY

Army Form C. 2118.

(Erase heading not required.)

Place	Date	Hour	Summary of Events and Information	Remarks and references to Appendices
STEENWERCK	4/6/17		The Battalion continued work under the orders of the 2nd Anzac Corps up to & incl. the 5th and then moved to BERTHEN on the 6th.	
BERTHEN to			Worked in the neighbourhood of BERTHEN until the 6th inst. The men then left BERTHEN on the	
DICKEBUSCH	30/6/17		6th and were forwarded by motor lorries to DICKEBUSCH and were then attached to the Canadian Corps	
STAPLE			for work on road construction etc. We left DICKEBUSCH on the 18th and moved to a camp	
DUNKERQUE			in the neighbourhood of CASSEL, continuing the work next day to LILLE's near STAPLE.	
INST DUNKERQUE			The Battn. remained in their huts until the 20th when we left for the coast, making for the	
			night of the 20th at fields near WORMHOUDT and proceeding next day to COUDEKERQUE	
			BRANCH near DUNKERQUE. Here the Battalion remained until the 23rd and when proceeded by road	
			and rail to OOST-DUNKERQUE BAINS and report billets on the dunes. The Battn was employed on road	
			construction, maintenance of coastal defences and maintenance of aeroplane, targeting R.E.	
			material for the formation of Dumps etc. The following reinforcements of Officers were received during	
			the month :— Lieut V. Ban. 3/6/17. Capt. J.A. Goss 14/6/17, Lt. H. Inn. 25/6/17 and Lt W. A. N. Fields	
			27/6/17. Lieut. I.O.P. Inglis rejoined the Battn from the TB Crystal Light Railway on the 7th and	
			was admitted to hospital on the 11th. Capt. T.P. Edmonds resumed the Battn from the	
			Canadian Rly. Construction Troops 24/6/17. Lt Colonel (Actively) (MC) returned from leave	
			20/4/17. Major T.B. Dowdeswell proceeded on leave	

Army Form C. 2118.

6 Welsh Rgt
Vol 25

WAR DIARY
or
INTELLIGENCE SUMMARY.
(Erase heading not required.)

Place	Date	Hour	Summary of Events and Information	Remarks and references to Appendices
OOST - DUNKERQUE - BAINS	1/7/17 to 31/7/17		The Battalion continued work on several ways, camouflage, road maintenance &c. Work was carried on under great difficulties owing to heavy shelling by the enemy and on the 10th, after an enemy attack on the East of the YSER, the whole of the camouflage screening constructed by one Company fell into the enemy's hands before it could be erected. On the 3rd July "B" Coy left for an unknown destination to be employed on important work under the supervision of C.R.E. On the 17th inst the Battalion moved by road to ROSENDAEL, proceeding on the 18th inst to ST POL-SUR-MER and on the 19th joined "B" Coy at LE CLIPON CAMP there to undergo a period of rest & training on the coast. The following Officers joined the Battalion during the month :- Capt St G Hawkins 14/7/17, Lt Pearson Bell M.C. 18/7/17. A draft of 119 O.R's arrived on the 3rd & various small drafts during the month brought up the total reinforcements to 181 O.R's for the month of July. The following Officers were admitted to hospital during the month:- Lieut DC Jones 8/7/17, Capt CJ Davies 15/7/17, Capt D McMorgan 17/7/17. Lieut Col L.O.S Poulton (D.S.O) rejoined the Battalion from the 8th Royal Berks Regt and resumed command of the Battalion on the 19th inst.	
ROSENDAEL				
ST POL-SUR-MER				
LE CLIPON CAMP				

CW Carter
LIEUT. COLONEL,
COMMDG 6TH (ISLAM) BN THE WELSH REGT

Army Form C. 2118.

WAR DIARY
or
INTELLIGENCE SUMMARY.
(Erase heading not required.)

Welsh 3/1 6 Vol 26

Place	Date	Hour	Summary of Events and Information	Remarks and references to Appendices.
LE CLIPON CAMP	1/8/17 to 31/8/17		The Battalion remained at LE CLIPON CAMP during the whole month with the Division, undergoing specialised training in preparation for contemplated landing operations. This training included training for & beyond fitness attack & defence schemes, some pioneering instruction, training in embarking and disembarking, and practice in calling a specially constructed section of sea wall. On the 25th Gen Sir H.S. Rawlinson Bart G.C.V.O., K.C.B., Cmdg IV Army's distribution medal ribbons to recipients on the 1st Division, after the distribution was made the occasion of a ceremonial parade & march past by the Division. Battalion Sports were held during the month with much success for 1st army, tug-of-war, cross country race etc., a Batt: Boxing tournament and Rugby football competition were also arranged. As a result of Hull Cup events "D" Company were declared winners of the Silver Cup & presented to Lt Col Company competition by Major O'Brien. Football matches were arranged with several other Battalions in Camp & several completed from the Battn took part in the preliminary stages of a Divisional Boxing tournament which is not yet completed. Lieut J.H. Beal took over command of "A" Coy on the 1st. 2/Lt O. Owen (15 days schools) struck off strength 5th. Reinforcements 2/Lt W.D. Evans 9th, Lt B.W.P. Davies 11th. 2/Lt G. Thomas 27th. Capt D. Davies pronounced "P.B." & struck off charge 10th. Capt 2/M Morgan & Lt G. Jones returned from hospital on 16th & 26th respectively. Lieut Col Carleton admitted to hospital 31st.	

L.C. Tosby Lieut Col
COMMDG 6TH (GLAM) Bn :THE WELSH REGT

WAR DIARY or INTELLIGENCE SUMMARY

Army Form C. 2118.

6 Welsh Regt.

Place	Date	Hour	Summary of Events and Information	Remarks and references to Appendices
LE CLIPON CAMP OOST-DUNKERQUE BAINS	1/9/17 to 30/9/17		The Battalion remained at LE CLIPON CAMP, undergoing training as in August until the 29th inst. During this period the recreational side of training received considerable attention and inter-section, with platoon and inter-Company football matches was arranged for the whole Battalion, with a view to ensuring that every man should play in at least one football match as part of his training. These matches proved to be of great interest but, owing to the Battalion having to leave the Camp at short notice, there was no opportunity to play off the "final" between the two winning sections. The same reason also caused the postponement of the "Final" of the Divisional Rugby tournament in which the Battalion has to meet the 2 Bn 4 Leicester Regt. The Battalion also held a very good record with the Divisional Boxing tournament having won three out of the four entries sent in, the remaining competitor being disqualified (with his opponent) for clinching. On the 29th the Battalion moved from LE CLIPON CAMP by road to DUNKERQUE, thence by rail large to ADINKERKE and thence by road to OOST-DUNKERQUE BAINS, re-occupying the same huts as before. Here the Battalion commenced work with the 42nd Division, on the buoying of Deceauville Line, erection of stables, track repair	

Army Form C. 2118.

WAR DIARY
or
INTELLIGENCE SUMMARY.
(Erase heading not required.)

Place	Date	Hour	Summary of Events and Information	Remarks and references to Appendices
LE CLIPON CAMP OOST DUNKERQUE BAINS	1/9/17 to 30/9/17		and maintenance, making wire netting tracks etc. On the 10th Lieut Col C.a.S Capston rejoined the Battalion from hospital. Capt H.b Hawkins was admitted to hospital on the 13th and returned on the 15th. Major Z.b Swaby proceeded on leave to England on the 22nd. On the 21st 2nd Lieut G.E. Soane (a former Coy Sergt Major of this Battalion) arrived as a reinforcement after having served a few days with the 15th Battn the Welsh Regt	

RCCBrabyn

for Adjutant
for LIEUT. COLONEL,
COMMDG 6TH (GLAM) BATT: THE WELSH REGT

WAR DIARY or INTELLIGENCE SUMMARY.

Army Form C. 2118.

(Erase heading not required.)

Place	Date	Hour	Summary of Events and Information	Remarks and references to Appendices
OOST-DUNKERQUE BAINS. ROSENDAEL. LAMBRE CAMP. BRIELEN.	1/10/17 to 31/10/17.		The Battalion remained at KENT CAMP working for the 42nd Division, in the neighbourhood of NIEUPORT BAINS. Consequent upon the 42nd Division relieving the 32nd Division in the NIEUPORT SECTOR, we moved on the 7th inst to BRISBANE CAMP, situated on the Dunes, near OOST-DUNKERQUE, and about a mile from our former Camp. Whilst here the Companies were engaged in maintainence of trenches and Covered Ways, Road maintainence, construction of Machine Gun Emplacements etc., in the neighbourhood of NIEUPORT. On the 18th inst we left BRISBANE CAMP to rejoin our own Division, now in the Fifth Army. We proceeded by road to ADINKERKE and were conveyed from there by Barges to ROSENDAEL. Here the Battalion was billetted until the 21st inst when we were conveyed by Bus to DAMBRE CAMP, situated about 2 kilometres North of VLAMERTINGHE, and on the VLAMERTINGHE - ELVERDINGHE ROAD. On the 23rd we moved forward from DAMBRE CAMP for work on roads under the XVIII Corps, the First Division having not yet arrived on this front. Headquarters were situated at G-HENT COTTAGES, just North of BRIELEN, and the Companies were in separate billets at some distance apart, "D" Company being the furthest forward with billets near SPAHI FARM (about 3 kilometres North of YPRES). Work consisted of maintainence and repair of Roads which, owing to heavy traffic, bad weather and enemy shelling were in a very bad condition. Lieut W.P.Dayson was wounded in action on the 13th inst and has since been evacuated to England. Captains C.J.S.Nicholl and D.M.Morgan were posted to the 19th Battalion The Welsh Regiment and proceeded to join that Unit on the 19th inst. The Adjutant(Captain R.C.Lindsey-Brabazon)proceeded to England on the 9th inst for a six months tour of Lighter Duty and Lieut A.E.I.Curtis took over the Adjutantacy, 2/Lieut R.F.Foster being appointed Assistant Adjutant to the Battalion. Capt C.J.Cowley proceeded on one months special leave to England 23/10/1917. During the month the following 2/Lieuts,who had completed 18½ months commissioned service,were gazetted Lieutenants:- 2/Lieut(temp Lieut) D.C.Jones,2/Lieuts Bell.J.N., Curtis.A.E.I.,Randell.H.L.,Taylor.H.P.,Lidgey.A.R.,Foster.R.F.,Rankin.J.,Evans.W.E., Napier.G.G.,Morris.E.G.,Statham.V.T.,Morris.M.,Abraham.J.G.,M.C.,Dayson.W.P., Knight.F.H.K.,and Bland.R.G.V.M. Lieut A.E.I.Curtis was promoted to Acting Captain as from 25/10/17 whilst acting as Adjutant to the Battalion. Lieut G.W.Richards to be Captain with prec.Nov.5th 1916.	

Lieut.Colonel,
Commanding,6th Battalion The Welsh Regiment.

WAR DIARY
or
INTELLIGENCE SUMMARY.
(Erase heading not required.)

Army Form C. 2118.

26C
1 sheet

Place	Date	Hour	Summary of Events and Information	Remarks and references to Appendices
BRIELEN. ELVERDINGHE. PROVEN.	1/11/17. to 30/11/17.		The Battalion continued work, first under XVIII Corps and afterwards under the 1st Division, now in the II Corps and II Army. On the arrival of the 1st Division, now in the II Corps and II Army, we resumed work with them on the 6th inst. The principal duty assigned to the Battalion was the upkeep of communications with the right of Divisional Sector. This necessitated the construction of a trench-board track from BELLEVUE to VALOUR FARM, across marshy ground which presented many difficulties and three tracks by varying routes were constructed in all. Having laid the track to the front line (which hereabouts is not much more than a series of shell holes), the Battalion furnished guides to conduct the attacking Battalion (the 1st Battalion South Wales Borderers) to their position in readiness for the attack on the 10th inst. Drainage work and improvement of road surface was also carried out in the neighbourhood of BELLEVUE. Repairs and improvements to Right Battalion Hd.Qrs, which had been damaged by shell fire, were carried out. Two Companies worked for the Divisional Signals on digging Cable trenches and burying Cables. About 1½ miles of trench were dug and cable laid, the trench being 2' wide and 6' deep, except in a few places where the ground was very wet. No.6.Track was repaired and a party was employed daily on the maintenance of this track. We were also engaged on the erection of 8-men shelters at STAGING CAMP. 57 Shelters were erected, camouflaged and trenchboarded. On the 24th inst a letter was circulated by Major-Gen E.V.Strickland, Cmmdg., 1st Division commanding the Division upon the way in which "Operations has been carried out in this Sector with a special mention to this Battalion for the long hours spent by day and night in the work of consolidation, and reconnaisance and subsequent guiding of the attacking Infantry, as a result of which, he considered, the achievements of the Division were largely due. On the 30th inst., the Battalion entrained at ELVERDINGHE for PROVEN where we rejoined our Division who had come out of the Line a few days before for a short rest. During the whole month hostile artillery was very active and we suffered casualties to the extent of 26 Other Ranks Killed and 66 Other Ranks Wounded. 2/Lieut H.B.Jones was wounded in action on the 12th inst., and 2/lieut E.G.Thomas on the 29th inst. 2/Lieut E.W.P.Davies was admitted to hospital (Sick) on the 25th inst. During this month the undermentioned Other Ranks were awarded the MILITARY Medal for "Bravery in the Field":- No.265948 Sergt.Hoare.F.H.W.. No.265471 Sergt(A/CSM)Pearson.W.J. No.266688 Pte Magness.H.	

R.G. Busby
Major,
Commanding, 6th Battalion The Welsh Regiment.

WAR DIARY or INTELLIGENCE SUMMARY

Army Form C. 2118.

6 Welsh R.
Vol 30

Place	Date	Hour	Summary of Events and Information	Remarks and references to Appendices
PROVEN. BOESINGHE	1-12-19 to 31-12-19		On the 4th the Battalion left PROVEN by road and took over from the French billets near BOESINGHE, Bn.Qrs being situated at ROUGE FARM; on the 7th Bn Qrs moved to RAYMOND FARM. During the month the Battalion was employed on:- Erection of Shelters by occupation by Reserve Battalion. Front Brigade. Construction of Trenchboard Tracks from CATINAT and FAIDHERBE CROSS ROADS. Maintenance of railway road and trench board track to CARRE DE LONDRES. Cleaning, widening and deepening the streams STEENBEEK, BROENBEEK and LOOBEEK. Placing of 17 Rummer Bridges across STEENBEEK and BROENBEEK. Erection of Shelters for one Company. XIX Corps Line in wiring &c. From the 21st that Company worked under C.R.E. Army Line, XIX Corps Area, in wiring &c on a new Army Line of Defence. Lieut. Col. Carleton was admitted to Hospital on the 1st & returned on the 16th. Capt. J. McRae (RAMC) proceeded to England on termination of engagement on the 2nd. Capt. J.P.R. Brownrigg (RAMC) joining the Batt. as M.O. on the same date (posted to Battn. 19th). On the 13th Capt. C. Brownrigg proceeded on leave to England, & his place was taken by Lieut W. Taylor (R.A.M.C.). Capt. I.R.E. Innes left the Battn. on the 9th to join R.F.C. 2/Lieut. E.W.P. Davies returned from Hospital on the 15th. Lieut G.M. Mills proceeded to England to join M.G.C. 19th. Lieut. Col. S.A.S. Carleton proceeded on special leave to England. 25/12/14 to 25/1/15. Lieut. L.P. Taylor rejoined the Batt. from Hospital 24th. Major L.C. Frisby took over command of the Battn. 1-15th & from the 25th during the absence of Lieut. Col. Carleton.	27C intell

L.C. Frisby Major.
Commanding 6th Batt. The Welch Regt.

1st Division

War Diaries

6th Welch Regt.

From 1st January, To 31st December 1918

WAR DIARY or INTELLIGENCE SUMMARY

Army Form C. 2118.

6 Welch Regt
Vol 31

Place	Date	Hour	Summary of Events and Information	Remarks and references to Appendices
BOESINGHE	1918. 1 - 31 January.		Three Companies continued work under C.R.E., Army Line, and were employed on Wiring Outpost Line, on drainage work and on clearing the LOOBEEK. The remaining Company worked under C.R.E., 1st Division on maintenance of road, railway and trench-board track, on clearing the STEENBEEK, and on erection of camouflage, up to the 7th when this Company joined the others in work under the C.R.E., Army Line. All four Companies were then engaged on wiring machine gun posts and on construction of belt of Wire in Army Battle Zone. Carrying parties from other Battalions, and a party of Belgian Engineers, worked with the Battalion during part of the month. On the 18th, 50 O.R. of this Battalion were transferred to 17th Battalion The Welsh Regt. and 50 O.R. to the 18th Welsh, their places being taken by a draft of men, classified B 1, sent up to replace them. Lieut. J. Rankin, who had been granted extended leave by the War Office on account of ill-health, was struck off strength as from 24.12.1917. Lieut. J. G. Abraham, M.C. proceeded to England, on joining the Tank Corps, and was struck off strength, 17.1.1918. Lieut. E. G. Morris proceeded to England on being accepted as an Observer, on probation, in the R.F.C., and was struck off strength, 22.1.1918. Lieut.Colonel Carleton, D.S.O., returned from leave 27.1.1918. During the month the under-mentioned Officers arrived as Reinforcements, together with 114 O.R: 2/Lieut. F. L. Cowen, A Coy. 17.1.18. 2/Lieut. J. Soar, B Coy. 18.1.18. " J. Cool, A Coy. 17.1.18. " J. T. Roberts, C Coy. 18.1.18. " H. J. Dunn, D Coy. 17.1.18. " E. Beynon, C Coy. 18.1.18. " W. J. Guy, D Coy. 17.1.18. " N. Wynne, D Coy. 18.1.18. " F. R. Ross, D Coy. 17.1.18. " K. L. Olsson, B Coy. 18.1.18. " F. Newlands, A Coy. 18.1.18. " R. D. Stevens, B Coy. 30.1.18.	

LIEUT. COLONEL,
COMMG 6TH (GLAM) Bn THE WELSH REGT

WAR DIARY or INTELLIGENCE SUMMARY

Army Form C. 2118.

Place	Date	Hour	Summary of Events and Information	Remarks and references to Appendices
BOESINGHE. TURCO CAMP HUTS	1 - 28 FEBRUARY, 1918.		Work was continued on an Army Battle Zone until the 10th. A Battalion garden for the production of vegetables was commenced on a suitable site near RAYMOND FARM, about half-an-acre being levelled and double-dug and prepared for planting. Indents for seeds, &c., were sent in but the Battalion had to leave before these were received On the 11th the Battalion moved by road to TURCO HUTS, East of the Canal, near PILCKEM. Work consisted of road and trench-board track maintenance, construction and erection of camouflage screening, constructing new pill-boxes and adapting old German pill-boxes in Army Battle Zone; and in digging trenches, constructing breastworks, &c under direction of 26th Field Company R.E. A new garden was commenced near the Camp, but owing to the numerous shell-holes and graves it was very difficult to find a sufficiently large plot suitable for a garden. In digging the garden several bodies of unknown soldiers were found, and in the camp the remains of an unknown officer of the East Yorks Regt., were found. A silver wristlet-watch, a bunch of keys and a collar-badge found with this body were sent to Graves Registration Unit as a possible aid to identification. In consequence of each Division now having to include a Pioneer Battalion, all Pioneer Battalions are now being re-organised on a 3-Company basis. As our personnel was considerably below our old establishment it was not necessary to transfer any personnel from the Battalion, but on the 26th inst. "D" Company ceased to exist as such, the personnel being merged into "A" "B" and "C" Companies on their return from work on that day. Capt. PEARSON BELL, M.C., O.C. "D" Company was attached to "A" Company. Rugby and Association Football Matches were held during the month between the Battalion and the 19th Northumberland Fusiliers, resulting in a win for the Battalion in the Rugby match and a win for the N.F's in the Association match. A Rugby Football match was also played between the Battalion and the 2nd Mons Regt., in which the Mons proved the victors by 3 points to nil. The following officers proceeded on 1 month's special leave to England, 1.2.18. Major L.C.FRISBY, M.C., proceeded to England for six months' tour of Lighter duty:- Lieut. A. R. LIDGEY, (1.2.18); Lieut. R.G.V.M. BLAND, (14.2.18); 2/Lieut. G.E.SOANES, (21.2.18). 2/Lieut. J. W. DAVIES was admitted to hospital, sick, 16.2.18. Lieut. F.H.K.KNIGHT was seconded for duty with Army Signal Service, 28.2.18. C W Carden Lieut.Col., Commanding, 6th Battalion The Welsh Regt.	

WAR DIARY
or
INTELLIGENCE SUMMARY

Army Form C. 2118

(Erase heading not required.)

16 Welsh R.
Feb 33

Place	Date	Hour	Summary of Events and Information	Remarks and references to Appendices
TURCO HUTS.	1918 MARCH 1-31		The Battalion was employed during the month on the following works. Maintenance & improvement of GROUSE TRACK, GLOSTER AVENUE, ALBERTA TRACK, WELLINGTON SWITCH, MOUSETRAP TRACK, HUBNER SWITCH & ST. JULIEN SWITCH, TRACKS "A" "B" & LANGEMARCK TRACK. These were repaired from LANGEMARCK - WINNIPEG Road forward to Daylight Limit. Maintenance of Plank Road from C.6.d.3.2 to D.2.a.2.3. On drainage & surface repairs of POELCAPELLE - TRIANGLE ROAD, LANGEMARCK AVENUE, BELLE VUE, CROSS CUT and MARK LANE. On construction and erection of camouflage screening at the TRIANGLE and the main PILCKEM - LANGEMARCK, BOCHCASTEL TRIANGLE ROADS. On the construction of Alternative Tracks for Track "A", GROUSE AVENUE, GLOSTER AVENUE and ALBERTA TRACK, including bridging the STEENBEEK and LEKKERBOTERBEEK where necessary. Arrangements made for the demolition of bridges over the STEENBEEK if necessary. The bridges over the STEENBEEK, BROENBEEK, STROOMBEEK and LEKKERBOTERBEEK were patrolled & maintained. "A" Company worked on Army Battle Zone throughout the month, & "C" Company worked on Support System of Forward Zone for about 10 days. The Regtl Bands of the Division (except Pipe Bands) were attached to the Battn for work & were employed from the 30th. on Battery Emplacement, revetting sides of gun-pits & constructing ammunition shelters. Work was continued on the Battalion Garden throughout the month, & various camp improvements were carried out. During the month the Battn. also maintained 5 Lewis Gun Posts for Anti-Aircraft work in positions selected by Dim. In consequence of the German Offensive in the neighbourhood of ST. QUENTIN, all leave was stopped on the 23rd. Leave had been running very well up to this time, men proceeding home after a period of from 9 to 8 months without leave. Several Football Matches & Boxing Contests were held with neighbouring Battalions during the month. Major L.C.FRISBY, M.C. returned from leave 4/3/18. Capt. A.E.CURTIS proceeded on leave 14/3/18, returned 31/3/18. Capt. V.DEER being O/Adjutant during the absence of Capt. CURTIS. The a/m Officers proceeded to England for a aircraft gun of lights. Lieut. G.G.NAPIER (14") Lieut. H.L.RANDELL (22nd) Lieut. F.W.ROBINSON being Assistant Adjutant in the absence of Lieut. FOSTER. Capt. PEARSON BELL, M.C. left for England, to join R.F.C. 26/3/18. During part of the month Lieut. R.F.FOSTER was employed as Dism.Officer, R.E. with the C.R.E. Lieut. J.ROSS was also employed as D.O.R.E. for a portion of the month. The following awards are received. No 265398 C.S.M. PRICE G. and No 265503 Pte DRISCOLL J. Belgian Croix de Guerre. No 265452 Pte EVANS B. (Military Medal), A.D.S.S./Forms/C.2118.	30 C Inter L.C.Frisby Major LIEUT. COLON. COMMDG 6TH (GLAM) BATT: THE WELSH REGT

1st Divisional Pioneers

1/6th BATTALION

THE WELCH REGIMENT (Pioneers)

APRIL 1918.

Army Form C. 2118.

WAR DIARY
or
INTELLIGENCE SUMMARY.
(Erase heading not required.)

Instructions regarding War Diaries and Intelligence Summaries are contained in F. S. Regs, Part II. and the Staff Manual respectively. Title pages will be prepared in manuscript.

6 Welsh R.
Vol 34

Place	Date	Hour	Summary of Events and Information	Remarks and references to Appendices
TURCO HUTS. BETHUNE. BEUVRY. SAILLY LABOURSE.	1st–30th April, 1918		The Battn remained at TURCO HUTS & continued work as during March, until the 8th. Instructions were received that the Divn would proceed to another area, to join the I Corps, First Army, & we left TURCO HUTS on the 9th. & marched to DE WIPPE, near ELVERDINGHE. On the following day we proceeded by road from PESELHOEK station by rail to CHOCQUES. On detraining at CHOCQUES on the night of the 8th the Battn marched into BETHUNE, & was billeted in the Esplanage. On the 13th we vacated the Esplanage in consequence of heavy shelling (all accommodation being above ground). Hd Qrs & A & B Coys proceeding to the Institution St Vaast & C Coy to the College des Jeunes Filles, all being accommodated in cellars. Whilst at BETHUNE work consisted of the construction of a new Army Line North-east of the town, running in front of the dock & astride the canal. On the 16th the Battn moved to BEUVRY. Here the Companies were employed as follows:- 1. "A" Coy were employed on the wiring by night of front line posts in the vicinity of CAILLOUX KEEP and ROUTE "A" KEEP. 2. "B" Coy were employed on the construction & fixing of 4 pontoon bridges over the	at Hd Qrs 31.C. 4 sheets

WAR DIARY
or
INTELLIGENCE SUMMARY.
(Erase heading not required.)

Army Form C. 2118.

Place	Date	Hour	Summary of Events and Information	Remarks and references to Appendices
LA BASSEE Canal,			9 on the maintenance of all roads & towing paths in the Divnl Area	
			3 "C" Company were employed on the wiring # by night of front line posts in the vicinity of ROUTE 'A' KEEP and LOISNE KEEP.	
			In addition, the Battn was charged with the manning of the LE QUESNOY – BEUVRY defences in case of attack.	
			On the 18th the Germans made a big attack on the Divisional front at GIVENCHY. This was preceded by a very heavy bombardment. A & C Coys who were completing their nights work in the neighbourhood of the front line were caught in the barrage & experienced great difficulty in returning to their billets. "C" Coy were for a time attached to the 1st S.W.Bor.s in the line helped to repel the attack. The enemy bombardment extended to the billeting area, gas shells being plentifully used, we suffered a number of casualties to men in billets, our total casualties during the day being 5 killed, 18 wounded, 10 gassed, 4 missing & 2 wounded but remaining at duty. Subsequently a number of men went to hospital gassed as a result of the gas shelling during the day.	
			On the 24th the Battn moved to billets in SAILLY LABOURSE & was employed on	

WAR DIARY
or
INTELLIGENCE SUMMARY.
(Erase heading not required.)

Army Form C. 2118.

'A' Coy. Wiring by night various posts in the VILLAGE LINE.
'B' Coy. Maintenance of all forward tramways, steams roads, tracks & water pipes.
'C' Coy. Wiring by night various posts in the VILLAGE LINE.
In addition we were responsible for the defence of the CAMBRIN and ANNEQUIN localities in case of attack, the 26th Field Coy R.E. coming under the orders of the Commanding Officer for this purpose.
On the 9th Lieut Colonel C.A.S. CARLETON D.S.O. left the Battn. to take over command of the 2nd Welsh. Major L.C.F. FRISBY M.C. assuming Command of this Battn. with Capt. C.J. COWLEY M.C. D.C.M. as Second in Command. On the 14th we heard that Lieut Colonel CARLETON had been wounded whilst with the 2nd Welsh.
Capt. H.C. HAWKINS was admitted to Hospital 6-4-18.
Capt. P.R. BROWNING (R.A.M.C.) was admitted to Hospital 20-4-18 & rejoined the Battn. 29th, his place being taken in the meantime by Major A.R. DALE (R.A.M.C.)
On the 24th Capt. R.C. LINDSEY-BRABAZON, M.C., rejoined the Battn. after a six months tour of lighter duty in England, Capt. A.E.I. CURTIS reverting to Lieut & becoming Assistant Adjutant.

Army Form C. 2118.

WAR DIARY
or
INTELLIGENCE SUMMARY.
(Erase heading not required.)

Place	Date	Hour	Summary of Events and Information	Remarks and references to Appendices
	26-4-18		Lieut. E.W.P. DAVIES proceeded to England, on transfer, to continue his medical studies.	
			The u/m Officers were wounded in action during the month:	
			2/Lieut. W.A.H. MILLS, 18-4-18	
			" F. ROWLAND 25th	
			" F. L. COWEN "	
			" J. T. ROSS 24th (Remaining at duty)	
			Lieut. W B EVANS 18th -do- -do-	
			No 60655 a/R.S.M. DAVIES, E, joined the Battn on the 4th. No. 264092	
			a/R.S.M. RYAN, T. proceeding to England on the 5th.	
			The u/m reinforcements were received during the month:	
			Capt. TOSSELL, I.G. (MC) 16th. Lieut. COOKE, H.E. 25th	
			" LEWIS, C.G. (MC) 19th 2/Lieut. WILLIAMS, T. "	
			" Lieut. DOUGLAS, H.A.S. "	
			also 80 O.R.	
			The following awards were received during the month:	
			265454 Sergt ILES, H.E. (military medal)	
			265492 Cpl (a/sergt) PREECE, J. -do-	

LIEUT. COLONEL
COMMDG 6TH (GLAM) BATT: THE WELSH REGT

Army Form C. 2118.

WAR DIARY
or
INTELLIGENCE SUMMARY.

(Erase heading not required.)

Place	Date	Hour	Summary of Events and Information	Remarks and references to Appendices
SAILLY LABOURSE	1918. 1-31 MAY		The Battalion remained billeted in SAILLY LABOURSE and being accommodated in cellars fortunately suffered but slightly from the occasional shelling of the village. Throughout the month "B" Company were employed on the maintenance of roads, tracks, tramways, streams & bridges in all forward areas of the sector. A great improvement was made on the overland tracks, which had been allowed to fall into bad condition, & all other works were kept in excellent condition. For the first half of the month 'A' & 'C' Companies were employed on the work of fortifying the SAILLY LABOURSE locality, the area being divided into two sections North & South, 'A' Company being responsible for the North, and 'C' Company for the South Section. The work consisted of the digging of new trench lines, the improvement of and additions to old trench systems, digging of "swallow" trenches in "Platoon Posts", a great quantity of wiring, & the strengthening of houses & "keeps" in the village itself. One Platoon from each of these two Companies was employed nightly wiring in front of the Support Line. During the last week of the month 'A' Company were employed on the construction of a breastwork parapet & parados to the LAUNDRY – ANNEQUIN Reserve Line	

WAR DIARY
or
INTELLIGENCE SUMMARY.

(Erase heading not required.)

Army Form C. 2118.

Place	Date	Hour	Summary of Events and Information	Remarks and references to Appendices
			On the 14th a scheme of training was commenced whereby one Platoon per Company should be under training each day. This arrangement was altered on the 30th when "C" Company commenced a seven-days' programme of 'Refresher' training the remaining Companies continuing work as usual.	
			On the 8th Lieut. A.E.I. CURTIS proceeded to England on transfer to Territorial Force Reserve for a period of six months.	
			Capt. H.C. HAWKINS returned from Hospital 10/5/18, & after inspection by A.D.M.S., proceeded to Base Depot on the 15th, as unfit for general service & was struck off strength 30/5/18.	
			Capt. P.R. BROWNING (R.A.M.C.) was admitted to Hospital 6th. & rejoined 20th. Capt. E. ROGERSON (R.A.M.C.) being attached to this Battn. as M.O. during the absence of Capt. Browning.	
			On the 16th, the two most recently joined drafts were inspected by Major General E.P. STRICKLAND, C.B., C.M.G., D.S.O. Commanding 1st Division.	
			2/Lieut E. BEYNON was admitted to Hospital 26/5/18.	
			Lieut. E. HAMMOND arrived as Reinforcement 10/5/18. & 2/Lieut. J.B. PAVEY arrived at Reinforcements Camp 24/5/18.	
			The n/m awards are recorded. No. 265726 Sergt. D. GRIFFITHS, D.C.M.	

WAR DIARY
or
INTELLIGENCE SUMMARY.
(Erase heading not required.)

Army Form C. 2118.

Place	Date	Hour	Summary of Events and Information	Remarks and references to Appendices
			Lieut. R.G.V.M. BLAND } Mentioned in Despatches. vide London Gazette of 24/5/18.	
			265905 Sergt. O.J. MAGGS }	

F.C. Nash
LIEUT. COLONEL,
COMMDG 8TH (GLAM) BATT: THE WELSH REGT

Army Form C. 2118.

WAR DIARY
or
INTELLIGENCE SUMMARY.
(Erase heading not required.)

Instructions regarding War Diaries and Intelligence Summaries are contained in F. S. Regs., Part II. and the Staff Manual respectively. Title pages will be prepared in manuscript.

Place	Date	Hour	Summary of Events and Information	Remarks and references to Appendices
SAILLY LABOURSE	1918. June 1-30		The Battalion remained during the month in the same billets in SAILLY LABOURSE. The work during the month was as follows:-	
			1 Company - Maintenance of Forward Areas.	
			1 Company employed on digging cable trenches & burying cable in Divisional Area.	
			1 Company training - the three Companies taking training in rotation, weekly.	
			2/Lieut. E Bryan returned from Hospital 6/6/18. 2/Lieut. W. J. Guy was admitted to Hospital 13/6/18. & 2/Lieut. J. T. Roberts on the 18th. 2/Lieut Guy being transferred to England 22/6/18.	
			Major C. J. Cowley, M.C., A.D.M. proceeded on leave to England 9th to 23rd	
			Lieut. C. Langer rejoined the Battn from Fifth Army Sniping School (previously attached to III Corps Intelligence) 28/6/18.	

LIEUT. COLONEL
COMMDG 6TH (SLAM) BATT: THE WELSH REGT

Army Form C. 2118.

WAR DIARY
or
INTELLIGENCE SUMMARY.
(Erase heading not required.)

Place	Date	Hour	Summary of Events and Information	Remarks and references to Appendices
SAILLY LABOURSE	1st to 31st July 1918		During the month the Batt: has remained in billets in SAILLY LABOURSE & has been employed on the following works:- (a) Maintenance of all forward roads tramways & drains in the Divisional Area. (b) The digging of forward cable trenches by night. Altogether the Batt: has dug about 5½ miles of cable trench since arriving into the Sector. A letter of thanks was received from the Officer Commanding 1st Division Signals on completion of the work. (c) The improvement of Locality Defences & construction of Anti-Gas Chambers for Locality &c. The Companies have taken it in turns weekly to have one week's refresher training. The weather has been too wet for much sort of doors recreation, but a certain amount of Rugby Football has been played. two pleasant games with the 2nd Welsh providing two wins. A very successful Sports Meeting was also held & a Boxing Contest. 2/Lieut J.T.ROBERTS returned from Hospital 11/4/18 Capt. G.W.RICHARDS was appointed Commandant, 1st Division Reception Camp & was struck off strength 14/4/18 Lieut. H.E.COOKE, medically boarded whilst on leave to England was struck off strength 15/4/18	

R.E. Bush
LIEUT. COLONEL.
COMMDG 6TH (GLAM) BATT: THE WELSH REGT.

Army Form C. 2118.

WAR DIARY
or
INTELLIGENCE SUMMARY.
(Erase heading not required.)

Instructions regarding War Diaries and Intelligence Summaries are contained in F.S. Regs., Part II. and the Staff Manual respectively. Title pages will be prepared in manuscript.

Place	Date	Hour	Summary of Events and Information	Remarks and references to Appendices
SAILLY LABOURSE PERNES	1-31 AUGUST 1918		During the greater portion of the month the Battalion remained in billets at SAILLY LABOURSE & were employed as follows:-	
			One Company on maintenance of forward tramways, tracks, roads & streams within the Divisional Area.	
			One Company on the reclamation & improvement of Forward Communication Trenches in Divisional Area, concentrating particularly on DAWSON STREET, QUEEN STREET, HERTFORD STREET, and BERKSHIRE ROAD.	
			One Company training & providing one platoon for the front line in the Sector held by the Right Battn. in the Line & under their orders.	
			The Companies changing over employment weekly.	
			A considerable amount of sport was indulged in, & a successful Sports meeting & Boxing Contest were carried out. The Battalion Rugby Team played off the Divisional Championship game with the 1st Glosters & won a great game by 13 points to nil. A cup & medals were presented after the match by Major-General E.P. Strickland, C.B., C.M.G., D.S.O., who watched the game.	
			On the 23rd the Battn. moved back to rest billets in the vicinity of PERNES	

Army Form C. 2118.

WAR DIARY
or
INTELLIGENCE SUMMARY.
(Erase heading not required.)

Place	Date	Hour	Summary of Events and Information	Remarks and references to Appendices
			and on the last day of the month entrained for ARRAS, to take part in the operations commencing on the 2nd prox., having for an objective the Hindenburg Switch Line.	
			The u/m Officers joined the Batt. as Reinforcements during the month.	
			2/Lieut. LLEWELLYN, E.M. 15th	
			" GEORGE, T.H. "	
			" MORRIS, W.R. "	
			" TALBOT, S.G. 16th	
			" JONES, J.E.S. 13th	
			Lieut M. MORRIS was struck off strength 14/8/18 "Retained in England by War Office."	
			Capt. P.R. BROWNING (R.A.M.C.) proceeded on leave to England 25th, Capt. W. STUTIAFORD (R.A.M.C.) being attached to the Battn. temporarily as M.O.	

R.C.Irish
LIEUT. COLONEL,
COMMDG 8TH (GLAM) BATT: THE WELSH REGT

Army Form C. 2118.

WAR DIARY
or
INTELLIGENCE SUMMARY.
(Erase heading not required.)

Instructions regarding War Diaries and Intelligence Summaries are contained in F. S. Regs., Part II. and the Staff Manual respectively. Title pages will be prepared in manuscript.

Place	Date	Hour	Summary of Events and Information	Remarks and references to Appendices
ARRAS area	1-30 Sept. 1918.		On the 1st of the month the Battn. left ARRAS and bivouaced in fields south of GUEMAPPE, at approximately N.24.d. (Sheet 51B) for the night, advancing next morning to the neighbourhood of CHERISY. Here the Division was in support to the Canadian Corps & successfully attacking the DROCOURT - QUEANT Line in the early morning of the 2nd. "A" & "B" Companies were attached to 3rd Brigade and 2nd Brigade respectively & were to be employed on "consolidation work" if necessary. "C" Company being in reserve. The Division however did not go into action.	
ST. QUENTIN area			On the 4th the Division "side-stepped", taking over from the 4th British Division. Companies were billeted in trenches in the neighbourhood of MONCHY LE PREUX, with Battn. Hd Qrs. at FOSSES FARM on the ARRAS - CAMBRAI Road (map reference N.10.b.10.4. Sheet 51B). Companies were employed on the construction of "dry-weather tracks" adjoining the ARRAS - CAMBRAI Road & on the maintenance of roads leading to the front line in ETAING and DURY. On the 7th the Battalion entrained back to the neighbourhood of HAUTEVILLE, & remained there until the 10th, when it entrained at AUBIGNY en route for the neighbourhood North of St. QUENTIN, & proceeded to VILLERS BRETONNEUX, leaving the latter place on the 12th by lorries for MONTECOURT & proceeding on the 14th to	

WAR DIARY
or
INTELLIGENCE SUMMARY.
(Erase heading not required.)

Army Form C. 2118.

Place	Date	Hour	Summary of Events and Information	Remarks and references to Appendices
CAULAINCOURT.			Forward roads were maintained & improved & dry weather tracks made in preparation for the push on the 18th. The operations were completely successful & the Companies immediately followed up the successful attack & repaired roads & tracks to the forward area for the first few days. From the 24th. to the 28th. the Battalion was employed by night upon the important work of erecting belts of wire in front of the captured positions, under orders of the respective Brigades. The task was somewhat hazardous but happily was accomplished with very few casualties. The work done proved to be of the greatest value, the belts of wire erected by the Battalion being largely instrumental in the defeat of a determined counter attack made against the 2nd Batn. K.R.R. Corps. After the further push on the 29th the Battalion moved forward to VILLECHOLLES & then to BERTHAUCOURT & Companies continued roads forward to new front line. Congratulatory messages were received from the General Officer Commanding-in-Chief, from the Army Commander & from the Corps Commander on the work of the Division in these operations, & the Divisional Commander also expressed to all ranks his gratification at the work done by all ranks.	
			The w/m Officers proceeded on leave during the month.	

Army Form C. 2118.

WAR DIARY
or
INTELLIGENCE SUMMARY.
(Erase heading not required.)

Instructions regarding War Diaries and Intelligence Summaries are contained in F. S. Regs., Part II. and the Staff Manual respectively. Title pages will be prepared in manuscript.

Place	Date	Hour	Summary of Events and Information	Remarks and references to Appendices
			2/Lieut. J.T. Roberts 15-9-18	
			Lieut. E. Longer 18-9-18	
			Capt. J.Y. Tazell M.C. 26-9-18	
			Capt. E.G. Lewis 28-9-18	
			Capt. V. Deer 30-9-18	
			Capt. L.E. Lindsey (b.of E. Padre) joined the Battalion 24-9-18. 2/Lieuts T.S.Thomas and R. Lewis joined the Batt. 26-9-18 & 2/Lieut R.G.Evans on the 30th. Lieut H.O.S. Douglas was wounded in action 29-9-18. 2/Lieut. K.L.P. Oleson whilst engaged on a daylight reconnaissance on the 30th found himself amongst the German advanced posts & same under heavy fire, he was obliged to shelter in a shell hole until night & succeeded in rejoining the Battn on the following day. The w/m officers were attached to 1st Batth Yorks & Lancs Regt 30/9/18. 2/Lieuts K.J. Nunn F.M. George R. Lewis & G. Y. R. Evans. The u/m awards are recorded:-	
			265454 Sergt. Geo. H.E. Turner, D.C.M.	
			266893 Sgt. J.R. D.C.M. M.M.	
			Casualties during the month :- Officers. O.R.	
			Killed in Action — 6	
			Wounded in Action 1 36	
			Wounded in Action but remaining at duty 1 4	

F.C. Tazell
LIEUT. COLONEL
COMMDG 8TH (GLAM) Bn. THE WELSH REGT

Army Form C. 2118.

WAR DIARY
or
INTELLIGENCE SUMMARY.
(Erase heading not required.)

Instructions regarding War Diaries and Intelligence Summaries are contained in F. S. Regs., Part II. and the Staff Manual respectively. Title pages will be prepared in manuscript.

Place	Date	Hour	Summary of Events and Information	Remarks and references to Appendices
BERTHAUCOURT	1.10.18		The Division having been temporarily withdrawn, the Battalion remained in the neighbourhood of BERTHAUCOURT and commenced a programme of training. On the 12th of the month orders were received to move up to BOHAIN, where the Battalion was billeted for five days and was enthusiastically received by the remaining French population, who were greatly excited at their release from German control.	
BOHAIN	6			
LA VALLE MULATRE	31.10.18		The Division moved forward again and attacked on the 17th and 18th with an American Division on the left and a French Division on the right. The Battalion moved forward on the 17th to D.6.b.9.5 (Ref. Sheet 57B) and on the 19th to LA VALLEE MULATRE, being billeted in this latter village until the end of the month. The Companies were employed on the repair of forward roads and tracks working as far forward as possible by day without direct observation. One Company was employed on the wiring of the front line posts held by 3rd Infantry Brigade	

Army Form C. 2118.

WAR DIARY
or
INTELLIGENCE SUMMARY.
(Erase heading not required.)

Place	Date	Hour	Summary of Events and Information	Remarks and references to Appendices

The u/mentioned Officers proceeded on leave to England during the month.

Lieut. J.W. Robinson 2/10/18   2/Lieut J.A. Jones 11/10/18   Capt. J.K. Bell 10/10/18

Capt. D.E. Jones 16/10/18   Capt. J.H. Russell M.C. 15/10/18

Capt. K.C. Lindsay-Brabazon M.C. 22/10/18   2/Lieut. J.B. Lacey 25/10/18

The Medical Officer, Capt. R.R. Browning (R.A.M.C.) was admitted to Hospital 30/10/18 and
Major H. Dillard (M.O.R.C., U.S.A.) was attached to the Battalion as Medical Officer 31/10/18.

2/Lieut G.C. Soanes rejoined the Battalion from a Six Months Tour of Duty in
England on 13/10/18 and was wounded in action but remained at duty on 19/10/18

2/Lieut W.R. Morris was wounded in action on 3/10/18 and rejoined the Battalion on 18/10/18.

2/Lieut J.W. Sons M.M. proceeded to England to join R.A.F. on 11/10/18.

The u/mentioned Officers were medically boarded and struck off the strength of the
Battalion

2/Lieut J.J. Roo   Capt. J.G. Toall M.C.   Capt. W. Dee.

The u/mentioned awards are noted.

266464 L/Cpl Orens 6A M.M.   50092 Pte Jones J. M.M.

LIEUT. COLONEL
THE WELSH REGT.

WAR DIARY
or
INTELLIGENCE SUMMARY.
(Erase heading not required.)

Army Form C. 2118.

Place	Date	Hour	Summary of Events and Information	Remarks and references to Appendices
LA VALLEE MULATRE LA GRAND FAYT SARS POTERIES HESTRUD BOSSU LEZ WALCOURT FRAIRE FLAVION ONHAYE	1/11/18 to 30/11/18		The Battalion remained in billets in LA VALLEE MULATRE up to and including 3.11.18, and was employed on the repair and improvement of forward roads in the Divisional area. On the night of 3.11.18. "B" Company and "C" Company were employed digging assembly positions to the South of CATILLON for the Divisional attack on 4.11.18. The Division attacked on the morning of 4.11.18 gaining all objectives including the high bank and CATILLON. The Battalion was employed reconnoitring and repairing all main traffic routes so far as the front line. During the afternoon of 4.11.18 orders were received to withdraw all parties from road work and to immediately take up positions in support to 2nd Infantry Brigade. The Battalion were in position by 2000 hours with Headquarters situated near L'HERMITAGE, east of the bank and Companies in the immediate vicinity. The Battalion was relieved on the night of 5.11.18 and returned to LA VALLEE MULATRE. From 6.11.18 to 13.11.18 the Battalion was employed on the salvage of road material in the area over which the 1st Division had fought	

Army Form C. 2118.

WAR DIARY
or
INTELLIGENCE SUMMARY.
(Erase heading not required.)

Instructions regarding War Diaries and Intelligence Summaries are contained in F. S. Regs., Part II. and the Staff Manual respectively. Title pages will be prepared in manuscript.

Place	Date	Hour	Summary of Events and Information	Remarks and references to Appendices
			their way during the preceeding week, and on the burying of the dead in the vicinity of the kind.	
			Armistice day on 11.11.18 passed off very quietly Courtplies being shot), a Battalion boxers being arranged in the evening	
			On 14.11.18 the good news was received that the Division was taking part in the advance into Germany and that the Battalion was to act as advance guard to the Division, repairing damaged roads to allow for the rest of the Division to move forward.	
			The Battalion halted at the following places, being welcomed by the inhabitants of each place :—	
	14.11.18		LA GRAND FAYT. 15.11.18. SARS POTERIES.	
	16.11.18		HESTRUD 17.11.18. BOSSU LEZ WALCOURT.	
	18-22.11.18		FRAIRE 23.11.18 FLAVION.	
	24-30.11.18		ONHAYE	
			On 17.11.18 a party of 2 Officers and 3 N.C.Os proceeded to England to bring back the Regimental Colours.	

WAR DIARY
or
INTELLIGENCE SUMMARY.
(Erase heading not required.)

Army Form C. 2118.

Place	Date	Hour	Summary of Events and Information	Remarks and references to Appendices
			The undermentioned Officers proceeded to England on leave :-	
			Lieut Col. L.C. Frisby D.S.O. M.C. 9.11.18. Lieut J.S.Greenwood 18/11/18	
			2/Lieut J.S. Thomas 27/11/18	
			Lieut A.L. Randall and Lieut G.G. Napier rejoined the Battalion from a	
			Six Months Tour of Duty in England on 28.11.18	
			Lieut W.B. Evans proceeded to Rouen to attend Lewis Gunner course	
			on 6.11.18.	
			The undermentioned awards are recorded :-	
			Lieut Col. L.C. Frisby M.C. D.S.O.	
			Capt. G.G. Lewis M.C.	
			No 261053 L/Cpl D.J. Thomas M.M.	
			L.C. Frisby Lieut Colonel	
			Commdg. 6th Battn The Welsh Regiment.	

Army Form C. 2118.

WAR DIARY
or
INTELLIGENCE SUMMARY.
(Erase heading not required.)

Place	Date Hour	Summary of Events and Information	Remarks and references to Appendices
MOUNT GAUTHIER HAID	1st-31st Dec 1918.	The Battalion moved forward again on the 1st of the month	
BAILLONVILLE		from ONHAYE passing through DINANT. Here a very good reception was	
TOHOGNE		given by the civilians. The Battalion proceeded in very good weather	
VILLERS STE GERTRUDE		On the night of the 2nd MOUNT GAUTHIER in the ARDENNES COUNTRY	
VAUX CHAVANNE REGNE		was reached and the Battalion rested there until the 7th.	
BOVIGNY SCHONBERG		From the 7th until the 23rd of the month the	
KRONENBERG		Battalion was moving forward practically continuously staying in billets	
SCHMIDTHEIM MUNITEREIFEL		for the night at the following places.	
STOTZHEIM		7th HAID 10th TOHOGNE	
ERSDORF + ALTENDORF		11th VILLERS STE GERTRUDE 13th VAUX CHAVANNE 14th REGNE	
		15th BOVIGNY 16th MALDINGEN.	
		On the day of the 16th the German frontier was crossed	
		and the Battalion Colour were carried unfurled as the Battalion marched	
		past the Divisional General.	
		17th SCHONBERG 18th KRONENBURG 19th SCHMIDTHEIM	
		21st MUNITEREIFEL 22nd STOTZHEIM 23rd ERSDORF + ALTENDORF.	

WAR DIARY or INTELLIGENCE SUMMARY

Army Form C. 2118.

Place	Date	Hour	Summary of Events and Information	Remarks and references to Appendices

The first part of the journey was favoured by good weather, which however broke on reaching BAILLONVILLE and very unfavourable conditions prevailed until reaching MUNSTERIEFEL. The troops marched very well throughout the trying conditions, and but little sickness was felt.

Her fullest at King WOODUL. On reaching ERIDORF the Battalion was billetted. H.Q. & "B" Company in the main village ERIDORF and A&D Companies in the adjoining village, ALTENDORF. Arrangements were made for the mens Xmas Dinner & were successfully carried out on Xmas evening.

The Officers & Sergeants Xmas Billet on Boxing evening.

At the latter end of the month demobilisation within the Battalion commenced and a large number of the Long Service soldiers were sent home.

A Supplies of Education within the Battalion was also organised and commenced on the last day of the month.

Lieut. R.G. Foster rejoined the Battalion from a six months Tour of Duty in England on 4.12.18.

Lieut. Buckland + 2/Lt. G.B. Storrs rejoined the Battalion with Reinforcements

Army Form C. 2118.

WAR DIARY
OR
INTELLIGENCE SUMMARY.
(Erase heading not required.)

Instructions regarding War Diaries and Intelligence Summaries are contained in F. S. Regs., Part II. and the Staff Manual respectively. Title pages will be prepared in manuscript.

Place	Date	Hour	Summary of Events and Information	Remarks and references to Appendices
Colour	on 7.12.18.			
			2/Lt. J.A. Jones having met with an accident in the future was proceeded	
			to Hospital on the 7-12-18.	
			Lieut. J.P. Grumwold rejoined the Battalion from leave. 13-12-18.	
			The undermentioned Non-commissioned Officers with ORs were taken on Strength	
			during the month.	
			2/Lt. H.J. Burn.	
			The undermentioned Officers proceeded on leave to England during	
			the month.	
			Major C.L. Corlett M.C., D.C.M.	
			The undermentioned Officer proceeded to England on 26.12.18 for Re-establishment	
			2/Lt. S.G. Tebbt.	
			Lieut. H.G. Randall was admitted to Hospital on 2.1.19.	
			In publish to the Orders Haig of Nov 8th the undermentioned were recorded	
			as having been special mention.	
			Capt. B.G. Jones. 202443 C.S.M. Owens R.	
			265647 L/Sgt Jeremy J.	

LIEUT. COLONEL
COMMANDING 19th BATT. THE WELSH REGT.

1919
WESTERN DIVISION
LATE
1ST DIVISION

6TH BN WELCH REGT
JAN-AUG 1919

6th Bn The Welsh Regt (Western Bn (Rovers))

Army Form C. 2118.

WAR DIARY
or
INTELLIGENCE SUMMARY
(Erase heading not required.)

JANUARY, 1919.

Place	Date	Hour	Summary of Events and Information	Remarks and references to Appendices
ERSDORF ALTENDORF			Transport "6" Company - ERSDORF; "A" & "B" Companies - ALTENDORF. The Battalion remained here during the month of January 1919, in billets as follows:- During the month Education was carried out by means of Morning Classes and afternoon lectures, and also factory progress made. Demobilisation which had been commenced in December 1918, had to be suspended on account of the strength of the Battn falling to the minimum allowed; at the same reason Leave had also to be minimised. Two hours a day Military Training has been carried out, and the afternoons devoted to Sports & Recreation. Towards the end of the month a Divisional Recreational League was started, and this Battn were included in a group with the Machine Gun Corps & Divisional Engineers. An inauguration march was played, the Battn Cup. taken had luck, were defeated by 3 goals to 1. This one is first organised attempt to raise a Batt Recreation Team, and it is evident that with more training an excellent side could be raised. The following awards were inserted in the LONDON GAZETTE SUPPLEMENT of 18/1/19 - 26782, CQMS. Morgan.D. 265903 Sgt. Majors O.J. 265259, T/S.M. Parks.C.J. 26789 CQMS. Nichols E.J. Major E.J. Cowley M.C. D.C.M. rejoined the Batn from leave on the 17/1/19. No. 4 J.S Thomas rejoined the Batn on the 13th January from the 1st Div Reception Camp, which he had been training for duty. Capt B.C. Lewis (C. of E. Chaplain) left the Batn for Div H.Qs on 18/1/19. Capt R.F Taylor & Officers & Myself on the 27/1/19 and 31/1/19 respectively on country roll Drafts to Demobilisation; afterwards 14 days Leave in ENGLAND. The following Officers proceeded on Ordinary leave during the month:- Lt. Col. N.C. Thoby D.S.O. M.C. 2/Lieut. E.M. Llewellyn Lieut. L.R. Buckland Lieut. E. Maynard " M. Morris. W.R. Evans Major H. Dillons. (M.O. R.C.O.S. Army att)	A of O

R.J. Cowley MAJOR
Commdg. 6th Bn. THE WELSH REGT

2nd Bn. The Welsh Regt.

Army Form C. 2118.

WAR DIARY
or
INTELLIGENCE SUMMARY.

(Erase heading not required.)

FEBRUARY 1919

Vol 44

Place	Date	Hour	Summary of Events and Information	Remarks and references to Appendices
ERSDORF ALTENDORF	1/28		The Battalion remained here during the month of February 1919 in billets disposed as follows: Battn Headquarters & Transport & "C" Company - ERSDORF: "A" & "B" Companies ALTENDORF. On account of the non-arrival of expected drafts, it was impossible to re-open Demobilisation. Educational morning classes were continued during the month; + also voluntary evening classes in special subjects. Military training was carried out for two hours per day, and the afternoons spent in Recreation & Sports - Football, Hockey, &c. The Battn. Rugby Team played several successful matches. On the 15th February, Lt.Col. L.C. Grisby, D.S.O., M.C., proceeded to ENGLAND for demobilisation; and Major C.J. Cowley, M.C., D.C.M., assumed Command of the Battn. Major S. Mann M.C. D.C.M. Royal Scots Fusiliers, joined the Battn from 1st Battn Royal North Lancashire Regt., on 28th February and took over Command as from that date. The following Officers proceeded in ordinary leave during the month; 2Lt. J. Williams; 2Lt K.L.P. Ollivier; 2Lt J.P.S. Jones; 2Lt Eur. Llewellyn; — Capt C. Langer proceeded on leave to PARIS.	

Shawn Major
Lt Col
COMM 5TH (GLAM) BATTN. WELSH REGT

WAR DIARY
or
INTELLIGENCE SUMMARY.

Army Form C. 2118.

Place	Date	Hour	Summary of Events and Information	Remarks and references to Appendices
ERSDORF & ALTENDORF	March 1919 1/23		From 1st March to 23rd March, the battalion remained in billets in ERSDORF and ALTENDORF. On 3rd March, drafts arrived from 15th and 19th Battns. the West Regiment (comprising, in total, 30 officers and 442 other Ranks. As a result of the arrival of these drafts, demobilisation was proceeded with speedily, commencing on 1st March. On 5th March a party consisting of Lieut Nightingale and 25 O.R. proceeded to HELLINTHAL to undertake duties of Area Commandant's Guard — which had originally been found by the 62nd Division. Further reinforcements from the 18th Bn. the West Regiment arrived on the 13th and 14th March — totalling 5 Officers + 200 O.R's; and more — from 9th Bn. Sheffield Regiment, on 16th March. On 14th March, B Coy. (less party at HELLINTHAL) moved to SCHLEIDEN to perform duties of Area Commandant's Guard, then on 20th March, a party of 1 Offr. and 51 O.R. proceeded on Animal Conducting duty from COLOGNE DEUTZ to Base, returning March. On 24th March the Battalion (less B Coy.) moved from ERSDORF and ALTENDORF to new billets at SECHTEM; and, on the same date, received draft of returnable men and volunteers from 2nd Bn. the West Regt., totalling 11 Offrs. and 314 O.R. Orders were received to despatch a party immediately to WESSELING to be at disposal of the Bürgermeister for purpose of Piquet, etc. This party, consisting of 1 Officer and 20 O.R. proceeded on	H2C Arthur
SECHTEM	24/31			

On account of the continual changes in the Battalion, due to Demobilisation, arrival of drafts, etc., – it was not possible to make very much headway in the matter of Educational Training. However, now that internal arrangements have been adjusted, it is hoped to make far greater progress than hitherto.

With regard to Sport, – this, too, has suffered very greatly, by reason of the changes referred to above. The Battalion Rugby Team was almost entirely reorganised on account of releasable players proceeding for demobilisation before the date of the Divisional Final which was twice deferred.

As a result, the team had practically no opportunity of combined practice before the match with Z Battery at COLOGNE on 30th March. However, the result (a 14 points to nil win) clearly demonstrated the Battalion's superiority despite the very bad weather conditions and state of ground.

Officers.

2/Lieut. I. Wynne returned from a Course at 2nd. Army Agricultural Farm, on 30th March.

2/Lieut. T. Williams proceeded on course at 2nd Army P. & R. T. School, COLOGNE on 14th March; returned 31st Inst.

Capt. C. Ranger returned from PARIS leave during the month.

Capt. R. C. Lindsey Brabazon, M.C. proceeded on BRUSSELS leave period 19th March to 28th Inst.

The following officers were posted to the Battalion during the month.

2/Lieut. C. Wyatt.
Capt. M.S. Morgan
Capt. W.B. Morgan, M.C.
Lieut. E.C.R. Mackadam
Lieut. D.M. Morgan
Lieut. Nightingale
Lieut. R.G. Fort, S.
Lieut. H. Miller
Lieut. B.M. Pritchard
2/Lt. A.T. White
Lieut. N.W. Thresh
Lieut. M. Evans, M.C.
Lieut. K. Williams
Lieut. J.A. Lake.
2/Lt. J.J. Ajax

Lieut. J.C.L. Vaughan, M.C.
Lieut. J. Pullein
Lieut. A.D. Grant.
Lieut. L.C. St.A. Lewis
Capt. A Roberts.
Lieut. W.C. Reynolds.
2/Lieut. J.S. Rouney.
2/Lt. W.E. Morgan.
2/Lt. G.T. Cattell
2/Lt. T.G. Parcell
2/Lt. J.H.G. Vaughan
2/Lt. E.H. Watkins, M.C.
2/Lt. L.G. Menhenick.
2/Lt. B. Sockett.
2/Lt. W.B. Gaughan.
2/Lt. T. Cow.
2/Lt. W.T. Rogers.
2/Lt. W.A.B. Price.
2/Lt. W.H. Knife.
2/Lt. H.B. Topless.
2/Lt. J.A. Jones

Lt. H.G. Docker, M.C.
2/Lt. J.A. Roberts, M.C.
2/Lt. W.G. Davies.
Lt. G. Davies
Lt. C.J. Read.
Capt. H.R. Perkins, D.S.O., M.C.
2/Lt. H.R. Evans, M.C.
Lt. T.H. Johns
Capt. F.C. Palmer.
2/Lt. W.H. Griffiths
Lt.Col. H.C. Rees, CMG, DSO.

(Continued) March, 1919.

Army Form C. 2118.

WAR DIARY
or
INTELLIGENCE SUMMARY.
(Erase heading not required.)

Instructions regarding War Diaries and Intelligence Summaries are contained in F. S. Regs., Part II. and the Staff Manual respectively. Title pages will be prepared in manuscript.

Place	Date	Hour	Summary of Events and Information	Remarks and references to Appendices
SECHTEM	24/31	—	The following officers proceeded on ordinary leave during the week :—	
			Capt. B.G. Jones	
			Capt. J.R. Bell, M.C.	
			Capt. M.S. Morgan	
			Capt. J.H. Russell, M.C., D.C.M.	
			2/Lieut. C. Wyatt	
			Lieut. C.E. Soames D.C.M.	
			Capt. C.G. Lewis, M.C.	
			2/Lt. G.T. Cattell	
			Lieut. R.T. Foster	
			Lieut. R.G. Port	
			Lieut. E.C.R. Mackadam	
			Lieut. D.W. Morgan	
			Lieut. H. Miller	
			Lieut. J.A. Bate	
			2/Lieut. W.E. Morgan	
			2/Lieut. F.J. Purcell	
			2/Lieut. J.W.G. Vaughan	

5th April, 1919.

J.C. Rum Lieut Col.
Comdg. 6th Bn. The Welch Regiment.

Army Form C. 2118.

WAR DIARY
or
INTELLIGENCE SUMMARY.
(Erase heading not required.)

Instructions regarding War Diaries and Intelligence Summaries are contained in F. S. Regs., Part II. and the Staff Manual respectively. Title pages will be prepared in manuscript.

6th Welsh
APRIL, 1919.

Place	Date	Hour	Summary of Events and Information	Remarks and references to Appendices
SECHTEM, Germany.	April 1919	1/30	During the month of April two Companies of the Battalion remained in Billets in SECHTEM, and continued training there. One Company remained on Detachment duty at SCHLEIDEN. As the Battalion had, during the month, arrived at what will be its settled personnel, on account of the demobilisation of practically all the remaining releasable men of the Battalion having been completed, a systematic programme of training was adopted, which it is expected will have satisfactory results in all cases. Educational Training was included in the programme above referred to, and good progress made. A proportion of each day was also allotted to Recreational Training; Inter-Platoon and Inter-Company Football Matches, Cross Country runs, etc., were arranged, and the keen interest evinced by the men in these competitions is sufficient incentive to warrant such schemes being continued. On the 14th the G.O.C., Western Division, presented Cup and Medals to the Battalion team which played in the Divisional Rugby Final. Orders were received to transfer direct through 2nd Brigade 90 retainable men from this Battalion to 53rd Battalion, Welsh Regiment, which transfer was duly effected on the 24th. Lieut-Colonel H. C. Rees, C.M.G., D.S.O., assumed Command of the Battalion on 4th April. Lieut H T O'Neill, R.A.M.C., was posted to the Battalion on 5/4/19 as Medical Officer. The following Officers proceeded on ordinary leave to U.K. during the month :- Lieut J P Greenwood 2/Lieut W H Knipe 2/Lieut W G Menhinick Lieut G F Nightingale Lieut Col H G Rees, C.M.G., D.S.O. 2/Lieut J S Thomas 2/Lieut A L Stirrat 2/Lieut N W Tharsh 2/Lieut W J Rogers 2/Lieut J S Romney Capt W B Morgan Lieut M Evans M.C. Major S.Mann, M.C.,D.C.M. The following Officers were struck off the strength of the Battalion during the month :- Major H Dillard, M.O.R.C.S. U.S.A., M.O. attached. Capt. H. R. Perkins, M.C. Lieut V T Statham Capt J N Bell, M.C. Capt H P Taylor Lieut E Hammond 2/Lieut R G Evans Lieut S L Buckland Lieut W C Reynolds 2/Lieut W R Morris 2/Lieut W B Gaughan 2/Lieut J E S Jones Lieut J Pullan Capt C Kenger Lieut J P Greenwood Lieut T Williams Maj G J Cowley M.C.D.C.M. Capt D C Jones Lieut R D Stevens Lieut G G Napier Lieut W P Evans Commanding, 6th Battalion, The Welsh Regiment. Lieut.Colonel,	H3C (sheet)

Army Form C. 2118.

WAR DIARY
or
INTELLIGENCE SUMMARY.

(Erase heading not required.)

HHC
1 sheet

Place	Date	Hour	Summary of Events and Information	Remarks and references to Appendices
SECHTEM, Germany.	May 1919.		During the month of May, two Companies remained in Billets in Sechtem, undergoing Platoon and Company Training. 1 Company remained on Detachment duty at SCHLEIDEN as Area Commandant's Guard etc. Demobilization of the few outstanding Officers, N.C.O's and men was carried out. On the 16th of the month the following attended a trip on the Rhine, organised by IX Corps :- 11 Officers. 189 Other Ranks. This was very much enjoyed by all. On the 29th instant, Lieut K.Williams was appointed Battalion Anti-Gas Officer. Throughout the month Education Classes were conducted daily, and good results were obtained. The following lectures were given:- 14th May. Lieut Reilly. Subject. "His treatment and experience as a Prisoner of War in Germany". The following Officers proceeded on leave during the month :- Capt R.C.Lindsey Brabazon.M.C. Capt F.C.Palmer.M.C. Lieut W B Evans. Lieut B L Pritchard. 2/Lieut I.Wynne. 2/Lieut C J Read. 2/Lieut H G Topliss. The following Officers were struck off the strength of the Battalion during the month. Capt A Roberts. Lieut E C R Mackadam. 2/Lieut G T Cattell. Lieut T H Johns, 2/Lieut J.G.L Vaughan M.C, 2/Lieut H R Evans. M.C. Major S Mann.M.C.D.C.M, Lieut W H Griffiths. Lieut R D Stevens. Capt C G Lewis,M.C. 2/Lieut J.S.Thomas. Lieut G Soames. D.C.M. Lieut G Davies. Capt (Temp Lieut Colonel) G.S.Brewiss. D.S.O.	

R.A. ?Simcan
Capt, Adjt for Lieut Colonel
Commanding, 6th Battalion, The Welsh Regiment.-

Army Form C. 2118.

WAR DIARY
or
INTELLIGENCE SUMMARY.
(Erase heading not required.)

Instructions regarding War Diaries and Intelligence Summaries are contained in F. S. Regs., Part II. and the Staff Manual respectively. Title pages will be prepared in manuscript.

Place	Date	Hour	Summary of Events and Information	Remarks and references to Appendices

SECHTEM Germany.	June 1919.		During the month of June 1919, two Companies remained in Billets at Sechtem, and continued Platoon and Company Training. "B" Company (with the exception of one Platoon) moved from SCHLEIDEN to ELSENBORN Artillery Practice Camp. One Platoon remained at HELLENTHALL. On the 3rd June, on the occasion of the anniversary of the birthday of His Majesty the King, the usual ceremonial parade was carried out for the purpose of this Battalion. Ceremony the 409 Field Company Royal Engineers paraded with this Battalion. On the 27th a party of about 200 All Ranks proceeded on a pleasure trip on the "RHINE", organised by the 2nd Infantry Brigade, and opinions expressed manifested the unanimous appreciation of these trips by all ranks. 2/Lieut W G Davies was appointed Battalion Educational Officer from 3rd June, vice 2/Lieut W.J.Rogers, who was admitted into Hospital. Educational work continued to form an important portion of the daily training, and is highly thought of by the men, who appreciate the benefits which they can derive from it. Throughout the month a considerable amount of time was devoted to recreational training, and the healthy spirit of rivalry and sportsmanship displayed during the progress of Inter-Platoon and Inter-Company matches is highly satisfactory. On the 13th June a lecture was delivered by Lieut King on the "Post Bellum Army". On the 23rd June Capt R C Lindsey Brabazon M.C., proceeded to the United Kingdom under orders to report to the War Office, and was struck off the strength of the Battalion. Special leave was granted on the 28th June to Lieut Colonel H.C.Rees, C.M.G, D.S.O., and Major E.J de Penthen y O'Kelly, D.S.O, assumed Command of the Battalion for the period of such leave. Eight days leave to LIEGE was granted to 2/Lieut W A B Price. 2/Lieut W J Rogers and 2/Lieut L.G. Menhinick were admitted to Hospital on the 3rd and 11th June respectively. The following Officers proceeded on Ordinary Leave during the month.-
			Lieut D Crew. Lieut A.Williams. Lieut A.D.Grant. Lieut H.G.Docker.
			Lieut R...Randell. 2/Lieut A.R.White. 2/Lieut I Wynne. 2/Lieut J A Jones.
			   2/Lieut J A Roberts,M.C.
			The following Officers were discharged from Hospital during the month, and rejoined the Battalion on the dates shown.-
			   Lieut J.H.Lake. 21.6.19.
			   " J.S.Romney 29.6.19.
			   " M.Evans,M.C. " "
			
			            Llewellyn Major.
			       Commanding, 6th Bn Welsh Regt.-
				45C

Army Form C. 2118.

WAR DIARY
or
INTELLIGENCE SUMMARY.
(Erase heading not required.)

Instructions regarding War Diaries and Intelligence Summaries are contained in F. S. Regs., Part II. and the Staff Manual respectively. Title pages will be prepared in manuscript.

Place	Date	Hour	Summary of Events and Information	Remarks and references to Appendices
SECHTEM. TRIPPELS- DORF.	JULY 1919.		The month of July was marked with very little, directly affecting the Battalion, which is worthy of narration, as standing out from the ordinary routine of "The Occupation". "A" and "C" Companies remained throughout the month at Sechtem. The Battalion Sports were held during the opening days of the month, and brought to a final on the 6th, resulting in "C" Company winning the "Bowen" Cup offered for the Company securing the most points. Without a doubt the best individual worker was Capt. M.S.Morgan of "B" Company, and his achievements in the final stages of the contest were distinctly outstanding, and merited the rounds of applause which were accorded him. The whole contest was typical of the sport loving nature of the British Nation as a whole, and its recognition and encouragement by the Army Authorities; and the German civilians who gathered in fairly large numbers must have thought similarly to the author of the remark that "The battle of Waterloo was won on the playing fields of Eton". An excellent opportunity of comparison of the "Sport" followed by the Welsh & German peoples was afforded, when on the 20th, the Civilian Gymnastic Clubs from Sechtem and surrounding villages assembled in this village to take part in a procession and Gymnastic display, which, while it was generally admitted was smart and well performed, was not the sort of work which appeals to Welshmen. The procession clearly typified the German love of the limelight, and had a distinct military aspect. Lieutenants J A Roberts, M.C and M.Evans. M.C.,and the following O.R's :- R.S.M.Probert. D.C.M., Cpl Rees M. M.M., L C Renshaw J. M.M., Pte Parkes J. M.C., represented the Battalion in the "Victory March" held in Paris on the 14th. The Battalion Colours were carried in the March by the above Officers. Three platoons of "B" Company left ELSENBURN Camp on the 19th, and took over Billets in TRIPPELSDORF, one platoon remaining at HELLENTHAL on Guard Duties. (CONT'D).	

Army Form C. 2118.

WAR DIARY
or
INTELLIGENCE SUMMARY.
(Erase heading not required.)

Summary of Events and Information

stand out in the recollections of those who were lucky enough to be in Eng land, to witness
The 19th July, the day of the English Official Peace Celebrations, will perhaps
them, but in the case of those of us who were in Germany on that day there will probably only
be a dim remembrance of a day's holiday and subsequent admiration of the glaring photographs
in the English Press of what happened at Home.

During the month closer attention was required to be paid to the Educational
part of the training, and although up to the present no Galileo's or Isaac Newton's have been
discovered in the Battalion not a latent Socrates brought to light, satisfactory progress
of a rather more elementary standard has been made, and it is certain that the efforts made are
appreciated by the men.

The military training during the month consisted of Schemes of a more advanced
nature, and special attention paid to Lewis Gun Work, Sentry and Outpost duties.

War Savings Sweepstakes were commenced in order to encourage the purchase of
War Savings Certificates, with good results. A fancy Dress Ball and Whist Drive
held during the month were ebranded popular. Prizes being presented by the C in C^g. Officer.

The Appointment of Adjutant to the Battalion was taken over by Capt H.L.Randell
on return from leave on the 3rd instant (vice Capt R C L Brabazon M.C. who returned to Civil
life at the end of June).

Command of the Battalion was relinquished by Lt Col H C Rees, C.M.G., D.S.O.,
on the 5th of July, and taken over by Lt Col A.G.Thomas, M.C. of the South Staffordshire Regt.

The Appointment of Second-in-Command to the Battalion was relinquished on 14/7/19,
by Major E J de Pentheney-O'Kelly, D.S.O, upon his being posted to 53rd Battⁿ Welsh Regt, and
taken over by Major J.A.Daniel, D.S.O., M.C., from the latter Battalion.

Lieut H T O'Neill, R.A.M.C., was transferred to 4th Battalion, Cheshire Regt, as
Medical Officer, and medical charge of this Battalion was undertaken by Capt. S.C.Nicholls,
R.A.M.C. 2/Lt W.G.Merhinick and 2/Lt V.J.Rogers remained in Hospital during the whole of
the month.

The following Officers proceeded on leave during the month :-
2/Lieut I. E. Ajax.   2/Lieut W.Hughes D.C.M.
"   E.J.Watkins,M.C.   " W.G.Davies.

[signature] Lieut Colonel
Commanding 6th Battⁿ, The Welsh Regiment.

Army Form C. 2118.

WAR DIARY
or
INTELLIGENCE SUMMARY.

(Erase heading not required.)

Instructions regarding War Diaries and Intelligence Summaries are contained in F.S. Regs., Part II. and the Staff Manual respectively. Title pages will be prepared in manuscript.

47C
1 sheet

Place	Date	Hour	Summary of Events and Information	Remarks and references to Appendices
SECHTEM. TRIPPELSDORF	August 1919.		From 1st to 26th of the month "A" and "C" Companies remained in Billets in Sechtem, and "B" Company at Trippelsdorf. Military, Educational and Recreational Training were items of duty followed by the Battalion during the early days of the month. A sad sequel to the Recreational side of the work happened on the 11th, when a Tug-of-War team of this Battalion were engaged in a contest with an R.A.F. team. No 46290, Pte Jenkins A of this Battalion collapsed during the pull, and upon examination by the Medical Officer was found to have died. He was buried at the FRIEDHOF Cemetery near COLOGNE. Orders were received for the Battalion to move to U.K., and although the amount of work thereby entailed was considerable, e.g. the return of requisitioned articles, horses, mules, transport vehicles, etc, on the 26th the Battalion entrained at SECHTEM. Whether the Battalion had created a good impression amongst the SECHTEM civilians, or whether the latter were glad to see the departure of the Troops, is not clear, but the civilians' demeanour at our departure would give one the impression that the English Troops were leaving to ward off invaders into Germany. Their mentality is without doubt remarkable. On the 27th the Battalion arrived at CALAIS, and embarked on the "Maid of Orleans" for Dover. In the records of this Battalion this date should be associated with the 28th October 1914, when the Battalion left England to try its prentice hand in the game of War. A fitting close to the history of the Battalion "On Active Service", is a glimpse at the scene at Calais. The feeling amongst the troops is slightly different to their previous experiences of this and other foreign ports, for now their work abroad has been successfully performed: the long anticipated "big ship" is at hand, England is nearer now than for a long time, and their only appears the prospect of realization of the well-meant wish "A speedy return", coupled with the hand shake that every one has experienced when first proceeding overseas. The following proceeded for demobilization :- Lieut J.A.Roberts. M.C., Lieut R.G.Lort. Captain M.P.McDonough. M.C., Lieut I.Ajax. Captain M.Edwards. R.A.M.C. joined the Battalion as Medical Officer 10/8/19. The following were admitted into Hospital during the month. Capt M.S.Morgan. Capt R.F.H.Duncan. Lt E.H.Watkins.M.C. Lt J.A.Jones. The following Officers proceeded on leave during the month.	

Lieut Colonel,
Commdg. 1/6th Bn The Welsh Regiment.

www.ingramcontent.com/pod-product-compliance
Lightning Source LLC
Chambersburg PA
CBHW081355160426
43192CB00013B/2415